D1505394

Modernity and Revolution
in Late
Nineteenth-Century France

Modernity and Revolution in Late Nineteenth-Century France

EDITED BY

Barbara T. Cooper
and
Mary Donaldson-Evans

DELAWARE

Newark: University of Delaware Press
London and Toronto: Associated University Presses

Associated University Presses
440 Forsgate Drive
Cranbury, NJ 08512

Associated University Presses
25 Sicilian Avenue
London WC1A 2QH, England

Associated University Presses
P.O. Box 39, Clarkson Pstl. Stn.
Mississauga, Ontario,
L5J 3X9 Canada

The paper used in this publication meets the requirements
of the American National Standard for Permanence of Paper
for Printed Library Materials Z39.48-1984.

Library of Congress Cataloging-in-Publication Data

Modernity and revolution in late nineteenth-century France / edited by
 Barbara T. Cooper and Mary Donaldson-Evans.
    p. cm.
   "Essays . . . selected from papers presented at the fifteenth annual
 Colloquium in Nineteenth-Century French Studies, held at the
 University of New Hampshire in October 1989"—Pref.
   Includes bibliographical references and index.
   ISBN 0-87413-447-1 (alk. paper)
   1. French literature—19th century—History and criticism—
 Congresses.   2. Modernism (Literature)—France—History—19th
 century—Congresses.   3. Literature, Experimental—France—History
 and criticism—Congresses.   4. Revolutionary literature, French—
 History and criticism—Congresses.   I. Cooper, Barbara T., 1944–
 . II. Donaldson-Evans, Mary.
 PQ295.M63M6   1992
 840.9′008—dc20   91-50645
                                                             CIP

Contents

6 Contents

Preface

The essays brought together in this volume were selected from papers presented at the fifteenth annual Colloquium in Nineteenth-Century French Studies, held at the University of New Hampshire in October 1989. Because that year marked the bicentennial of the French Revolution and the centennial of *L'Exposition universelle*, the conference organizers sought to give coherence to the program by adopting the year 1889 as a focal point for looking both forward and backward in French literature, history, art, and science of the nineteenth century.

Despite the fact that 1889 is not usually considered *une année-charnière* (a "watershed" year) in the same sense that 1830 and 1857 generally are in literature, or 1830, 1848, and 1870 are in history, the organizers felt that it might indeed represent a pivotal moment in French life and letters. To be sure, no new literary movements occupied center stage in 1889, nor did any major political upheaval dominate the news. Yet this was the first time since the Revolution itself that *le 14 juillet* was officially celebrated as the French national holiday. This event, in conjunction with the opening of the *Exposition universelle* with its monumental Eiffel Tower, its Hall of Machines, and its exhibits of the French colonies, clearly put a Janus-like face on that year. On the one hand, by elevating the anniversary of the fall of the Bastille to the status of the official national holiday, Third Republic France sought to affirm its identity and its place in French history by way of a symbolic link between itself and a certain ideological vision of the past. On the other hand, it simultaneously proclaimed its place in the "modern" world through the architectural structures and the exhibits erected for the *Exposition universelle*.

Stubbornly resistant to categorization, the essays published in this volume do, as a group, concern themselves with modernism and/or revolution, in the broadest sense of those two terms. The authors and artists whose works are analyzed here sought in highly self-conscious ways to revolutionize the traditional practices of their art. In their quest for new forms of expression that would somehow reflect the spirit of the times in which they lived, they experimented relentlessly, at times looking forward for their inspiration, and at times seeking it in the past. It is this experimentation and its cultural implications that the studies assembled here attempt to elucidate.

Although we have grouped the essays in this volume under three distinct headings (*"Fins-de-siècle,"* **"Voices and/in Dialogue,"** **"History and its Texts"**), we do not mean to suggest that they can or should be defined by any one category or context. In his study included here, Peter Schofer has suggested that Baudelaire's *Le Spleen de Paris* may be read as "a deck of cards which can be continuously shuffled and where, with each shuffle, a new context is created." We urge readers to treat the texts in this volume in a similar manner, to work forward and backward through the studies presented here in ways that seem most fruitful to them personally.

Our own first heading, *"Fins-de-siècle,"* brings together a group of articles that, each in its own way, contributes to the ongoing reassessment of the writings produced during the 1880s and 1890s. Each of the texts examined reveals the late nineteenth century's interest in the darker sides of our aesthetic, moral, or scientific imagination, and each of the essays allows us to discover provocative parallels between the end of the last century and those of our own so-called postmodern times. Proceeding chronologically, we begin this section with two studies devoted to Huysmans's *"bréviaire de la décadence," A rebours.*

In Dean de la Motte's view, *A rebours* is both "modernist" and "revolutionary", modernist in the sense that it eschews character development, causality, and teleology as structuring devices, and revolutionary in the etymological sense because it is a rebellion, in this case against "the mimetic claims of Naturalism and the representational pretensions of democracy." According to de la Motte, des Esseintes's disdain for and flight from the world must be read as more than a withdrawal from bourgeois society. The character's drama is the "final, exhausted exercise of democratic individualism itself."

Roy Jay Nelson examines Huysmans's novel from another perspective. For him, despite the work's apparent incoherence, *A rebours* derives a type of unity from its consistent use of irony. Nelson asks, "[W]hat sort of 'script' can readers construct that will allow for a character's belief in materialistic determinism and his search for the marvelous, that can contain a 'natural' penchant for the artificial?" The answer, he suggests, is based on the model of sacrilege, which perversely allows one to profane a belief system only after having first accepted it.

Like Huysmans, Villiers de l'Isle-Adam was fascinated by the power of artifice. In Jeffrey Wallen's view, the importance of Villiers's *L'Eve future* derives less from its uncovering of various forms of illusion than from its "simulacral logic" which relies on an ideology based upon gender differences. For Wallen, "sexual difference both resists and instigates the entire problematic of difference in *L'Eve future*, but it cannot finally determine its outcome."

Focusing on *fin-de-siècle* technology and its impact on French literature, Franc Schuerewegen shows how the aesthetico-philosophical problem of the "here and now," which we often imagine to be a product of our own advanced "teletechnological" age (the term is Lyotard's), had already preoccupied such writers as Villiers and Jules Verne. Schuerewegen's thoughtful and provocative analysis of *L'Eve future* and Verne's *Le Château de Carpathes* invites us to rethink both Villiers's much touted antipositivism and Verne's reputation as a spokesman for scientific progress.

In the final essay in this section, Will McLendon argues that through the seemingly "perverse" characters of such novels as *La Marquise de Sade* and *Les Hors-nature*, Rachilde may have been taking aim at the monstrous abuses of bourgeois values in late nineteenth-century French society. McLendon notes that "the more outrageous the abuse seems to Rachilde, the more she ups the ante by inventing characters and aberrations that for her time were definitely beyond the pale."

The second section of this volume, **"Voices and/in Dialogue,"** ranges more broadly across genres than the first set of essays. It derives its unity not from a single artistic form, but from a common focus on voice and dialogue. This section opens with Karen Erickson's examination of prophetic utterances in *Les Trois contes*. Erickson studies the effect of such utterances on narrative structure, their relationship to irony, and their role as a vehicle for social criticism. She sheds new light on the role of Félicité's parrot Loulou and convincingly demonstrates that prophetic voices are one of the threads that tie Flaubert's three tales together.

What do art and fashion have in common and what connection is there between the notorious courtesan Cora Pearl and the poet Charles Baudelaire? Sima Godfrey answers those questions when she juxtaposes writings on makeup by Baudelaire and Gautier with their more familiar works on aesthetics. Her study of these texts reveals unsuspected connections between *une toilette savamment composée* and Baudelaire's preference for the artificial rather than the natural.

The next two studies focus on another facet of Baudelaire's art. In a sensitive reading of Baudelaire's prose poems, Edward Kaplan demonstrates how *Le Spleen de Paris* is unified by the narrator's search for dialogue. For Kaplan, Baudelaire is "a self-critical *flâneur* who repeatedly attempts to reconcile his aesthetic and ethical drives, . . . to harmonize his solitary quest for perfect beauty with his desire to overcome social alienation." Peter Schofer's reading of Baudelaire's "L'Etranger," the first text in Le Spleen de Paris, attempts to uncover the dialogical tension between contexts and encoding through a study of the way in which Baudelaire creates open contexts which allow his prose poems to float "like clouds" and thus to avoid the "death" of a finalized context.

In the final essay in this section, William Sharpe turns his attention to the genre of the "nocturne" which rose to prominence in poetry and painting at the end of the nineteenth century. Sharpe shows how this particular artistic form allowed its practitioners to explore both public and private concerns, both the city and the psyche. The "widespread fascination with night and the nocturne" was, he argues, "an important strand in the fabrication of Modernism" on both sides of the English Channel. So, too, was the dialogue between the arts that he so clearly outlines in his study.

The last section of this collection, **"History and its Texts"**, examines the ways in which the past is "written" by literary historians, governments, novelists, and polemicists. This section begins with an essay by Jean-Jacques Thomas. In attempting to understand the relative "popularity" of such writers as Hugo, Vallès, and Zola, Thomas finds it useful to examine their use of language. He contends that nineteenth-century "revolutionary" texts of counter-discourse participate in a conception of language based on an implicit belief in semiological principles which impart teleological value to the linguistic sign. Realism ought thus to be distinguished, not from idealism, but from nominalism, he suggests.

Charles Stivale studies representations of the Commune in Zola's La Débâcle and Vallès's L'Insurgé, applying the Deleuzian concept of fêlure ("fissure") in his analysis of the former, and examining the latter using a different mode of analysis, that of le plissement ("folding," also derived from Deleuze). These concepts allow Stivale to show the contrasting ways in which Zola and Vallès contextualized history.

In the final essay in this volume, Willa Silverman explores the links between fin-de-siècle anti-semitism and occultism. Silverman finds considerable evidence to support the thesis that for some late nineteenth-century polemicists, the Jews were associated with invisible and malevolent forces. Taking her examples from selected texts by Edouard Drumont, Gaston Méry and Gyp, Silverman shows how that association betrays a fear not only of Jews, but also of the secular dogma of scientific materialism.

Silverman's essay brings us back to the darker side of the late nineteenth-century French imagination and to the question raised, in Schuerewegen's study and elsewhere, about the similarities between our own times and those of our forebears. We are led to wonder whether scholars at the end of the next century will see parallels between Jean-Marie Le Pen and Edouard Drumont, for example, or whether they will compare the ontological uncertainties apparent in Villiers's *L'Eve future* and Verne's *Château des Carpathes* to those revealed in the recent Paul Verhoeven films *RoboCop* and *Total Recall*. We can also ask ourselves whether the late twentieth century's search for alternative realities as well as its substitution of "electronic interfacing" for more direct forms of human contact will be seen as continuations of des Esseintes's attempt to withdraw from the world of "natural" experiences. Will someone examine our *fin de siècle's* perspective on "perversities" alongside those of Rachilde and her contemporaries? Is the ironic mode of sacrilege, which Nelson uses to discover the underlying unity in *A rebours*, in fact more broadly characteristic of the artistic and cultural artifacts of our own and Huysmans's age than we have hitherto suspected? Must we first embrace the past, albeit a past of our own making, before we can construct our future? One does not need to be endowed with a prophetic vision to predict that these and other questions surely will occur to twenty-first-century scholars. It is our hope that they, and our contemporaries, might find the elements of a response to those queries in the essays published here.

Acknowledgments

The editors of this volume owe a debt of thanks to many people for their support and generosity. We would especially like to acknowledge the help of Professor Grover E. Marshall, co-host of the Fifteenth Annual Colloquium in Nineteenth Century French Studies, for his invaluable assistance early in the process of screening the essays submitted for publication here. We also owe an immense debt of gratitude to Ms. Barbara A. Armstrong, secretary of the Department of French and Italian at the University of New Hampshire, for her untiring help in preparing the manuscript of this volume for publication. Juliette Rogers and Ann Willeford each translated an essay published here and we thank them for the long hours and the care that they brought to those two richly dense texts. We are also pleased to acknowledge the financial contributions of the University of New Hampshire's Undesignated Gifts Fund, the UNH Center for the Humanities, and the College of Liberal Arts of the University of New Hampshire in support of the Fifteenth Annual Colloquium in Nineteenth-Century French Studies. Last, but by no means least, we wish to thank our families for their patience and understanding during our long-distance collaboration on this project. Perhaps now they can use the phone again.

★   ★   ★

Permission from the following is hereby acknowledged: The University of California Press, to use material published in *Paul Verlaine: Selected Poems*, edited/translated by C. F. MacIntyre, copyright 1948 by The Regents of the University of California; Angel Flores, ed. *An Anthology of French Poetry from Nerval to Valéry*, to quote from a translation of Corbière's "Paris nocturne."

Credits for illustrations are as follows: Pissarro: *Boulevard Montmartre at Night*, ca. 1897, the National Gallery, London; Degas: *Femmes devant un café le soir*, 1887, Cliché des Musées Nationaux, Paris; Seurat: *Parade de cirque*, 1887–88, the Metropolitan Museum of Art, Bequest of Stephen C. Clark, 1960 (61.101.17); Degas: *La Chanson du chien*, ca. 1875–78, private collection; Whistler, *Old Battersea Bridge*, 1872–75, Tate Gallery Publications, London. Permission to use the cover illustration, Servando: *Vue générale de l'Exposition universelle de 1889* (lithograph), was provided by Les Musées de la Ville de Paris.

Modernity and Revolution
in Late
Nineteenth-Century France

PART I
Fins-de-siècle

Writing against the Grain: *A rebours*, Revolution, and the Modernist Novel

DEAN DE LA MOTTE

Something of a consensus has been reached among recent critics of Huysmans's *A rebours* (1884), placing it within the ashes of Naturalism from which the Modernist novel was born.[1] Those interested in the explosive mixture of reaction and revolution in *fin-de-siècle* narrative have rightly seen *A rebours* as a key text in our understanding of the elements of both continuity and rupture in Modernist fiction. My intention here is to view the findings of more detailed structural and narratological studies in sociological and historical perspective.

A popular historian has recently repeated, in his history of the French Revolution, the notion that "the creation of the modern political world coincided precisely with the birth of the modern novel."[2] If there is any truth to this, then this year, as we look back to 1789 through the pince-nez of the 1880s, *A rebours* takes on even more revolutionary significance. Yet as the etymology of the word "revolution" itself suggests, an equal measure of reaction informs Huysmans's novel. *A rebours* rebels at once against the mimetic claims of Naturalism and against the representational pretensions of democracy. The text is not, however, a simple revolt against or withdrawal from bourgeois society. The non-Aristotelian "drama" enacted within the walls of Fontenay, between the superimposed beginning and end of the novel—which is to say between the covers of *A rebours*—is the final, exhausted, exercise of democratic individualism itself. Des Esseintes's noble lineage constitutes only a pretext for his hatred of late nineteenth-century democracy, a fact that somewhat obscures the organic relation of the character's complaints to the society he disdains and flees.

Huysmans's *"Préface écrite vingt ans après le roman"* ("Preface written twenty years after the novel") is particularly instructive in its presentation of the context of the writing of the novel. The writer's description of his situation is shot through with the language of closure—so central to recent studies of nineteenth- and twentieth-

19

century narrative—and claustration, the primary structural and thematic obsession of *A rebours* itself, as Victor Brombert has pointed out.[3] The very figures used to describe the crisis of Naturalism become the central, positive, poetic language of the novel: circularity, stasis, enclosure. Naturalism is described as *"piétinant sur place"*[4] ("marking time"), that it *"s'essoufflait à tourner le meule dans le même cercle"*[5] ("was tiredly turning the grindstone in the same old circle"). Huysmans and others began to wonder *"si le naturalisme n'aboutissait pas à une impasse et si nous n'allions pas bientôt nous heurter contre le mur du fond"* ("if Naturalism had not reached an impasse and if we were not about to run against a final wall"). *"Je cherchais vaguement,"* he continues, *"à m'évader d'un cul-de-sac où je suffoquais . . ."*[6] ("I was vaguely groping for an escape from the dead end where I was suffocating"). The paradoxical coexistence of claustrophobia and claustrophilia is another Modernist trait, particularly in writers such as Kafka and Beckett. The divorce between society and art so typical of *fin-de-siècle* aestheticism allows Huysmans (and, for that matter, des Esseintes) to believe simultaneously in societal degeneration and artistic regeneration. In *A rebours*, the former in fact makes possible the latter, as the following well-known quotation suggests:

> There were many things that Zola could not understand. First there was my need to open windows, to flee an environment where I was gasping for air. Then there was my desire to shake off old habits, to break out of the limits of the novel . . . What struck me most at the time was the importance of doing away with traditional plot, indeed even romance and women altogether, and of focusing entirely on a single character. Finally, I wished at all costs to create something utterly new.[7]

Huysmans, in a typically modernist gesture, flees the suffocation of traditional closure for the hermetic enclosure of des Esseintes's experiences and *expériences* (experiments) at Fontenay. *A rebours* resembles the "open" Modernist text, as critics have pointed out, in its eschewal of causal progression, traditional character development and teleology. But both the shape of the text and the concerns of narrator and protagonist alike are resolutely closed.

The closure of traditional teleological narrative is grounded, as D. A. Miller and others have suggested, in the possibility of a reopening of experience.[8] Such a text ends where life takes up after the resolution of conflict or crisis. Modernist narrative, including *A rebours*, begins where teleological narrative stalls. Rather than an untying of the traditional knot—the *dénouement*—*A rebours* is a static binding, a word singularly appropriate for the character who has his walls bound like books. What better to symbolize the progressive movement from nature to society, society to individual and, finally, from individual to text, the ultimate artifice?

Des Esseintes himself, the last of a long line and thus an incarnation of nonlinear development, wishes the same fate on *"les générations nouvelles"*[9] ("the younger generations") he loathes. The stasis or stalling of narrative is then at once an act of revolutionary nihilism, or even suicide, and a reactionary gesture toward transcendence. Brombert has demonstrated that for Huysmans "the notion of salvation proves inseparable from claustrophilia,"[10] and I wish only to suggest that such claustrophilia is the direct product of the narrative claustrophobia, or dread of closure, that haunts fiction from Flaubert to Beckett and beyond. The two are inseparable; as des Esseintes realizes, his *"thébaïde raffinée"*[11] ("refined refuge") holds its attraction only as long as it remains near Paris, *"assez près cependant pour que cette proximité de la capitale le confirmât dans sa solitude"*[12] ("yet still close enough to strengthen him in his solitude").

How far have we strayed, then, from the theme of revolution? Not very, for the paradox of fictional closure sketched above is intimately tied to the fate of postrevolutionary individualism and the idea of progress, and in a way duplicates the very mechanism of revolution itself. As Louis Dumont has pointed out, the *Déclaration des droits de l'homme et du citoyen* "marks in a way the apotheosis of the individual."[13] But between the first, still royalist, *Déclaration* of 1789 and the final draft of the 29 May 1793 version, *égalité* joins, and finally takes precedence over, *liberté* in the enumeration of substantive rights listed in Article II.[14] If the tension inherent in any democracy between individual liberty and social equality generates much of the thematic material and teleological form of nineteenth-century narrative, then some continuity can be given to *A rebours*'s place in literary history. With the homogenization of society, the individual can only turn upon himself for nourishment, as des Esseintes does: *"Il vivait sur lui-même, se nourrissait de sa propre substance, pareil à ces bêtes engourdies, tapies dans un trou, pendant l'hiver"*[15] ("He fed upon himself, was nourished by his own flesh, like those animals that hibernate in a hole for the winter"). It is only a small step from here to Beckett's ditches, garbage cans, enormous jars, and other forms of enclosure or immobilization.

Huysmans's inward turn, however, is not accomplished without some elaborate props. Des Esseintes's much-discussed obsession with artifice—*"Au reste, l'artifice paraissait à des Esseintes la marque distinctive du génie de l'homme"*[16] ("For that matter artifice seemed to des Esseintes the distinctive sign of man's genius")—reproduces the anthropological structure of individualism itself. Holism, as Dumont defines it, is "an ideology that valorizes the social whole and neglects or subordinates the human individual," while individualist ideology "valorizes the individual . . . and neglects or subordinates the social whole."[17] "Artificialism" is precisely Dumont's word for the structure of postrevolutionary individualism; but des Esseintes, in his sequestered quest for self-fulfillment, rejects even the conditions that make such a social contract possible. The *Bildungsroman* was generated in part by a belief (albeit never unconditional) in the perfectibility of the individual and, by extension, in societal progress. When des Esseintes rejects progress, linear development naturally becomes unthinkable. It is hardly surprising, then, that he chooses not to undertake his journey to London: *"A quoi bon bouger, quand on peut voyager si magnifiquement sur une chaise?"*[18] ("What's the point of moving, when one can travel so magnificently in a chair?") A real—or if you like "mimetic"—journey would only, as he goes on to say, end in disillusionment.

From our perspective, of course, Huysmans's choice of *"désillusion"* here is thick with irony, and des Esseintes's flight from reality is deliciously double-edged. On the one hand, he knows what Emma Bovary never learns, that desire is far more desirable than possession. On the other, his refusal reads as a subtle Modernist critique of Naturalism's mimetic delusions.

Modernist plotting and characterization themselves have traditionally been likened to myth. In Joseph Frank's now classic formulation, fiction's move into Modernism is:

> the transformation of the historical imagination into myth—an imagination for which historical time does not exist, and which sees the actions and events of a particular time only as the bodying forth of eternal prototypes.[19]

Huysmans anticipates such developments, but my purpose here has been to underscore how much the textual strategies of *A rebours*—largely identical to the concerns of both its narrator and protagonist—owe to what I see as a shift from a progress-centered to a postprogressive (and in this sense already "postmodern") fictional paradigm. Huysmans's resounding rejection of progress, which sums up a tradition of discontent stretching at least as far back as Rousseau and Goethe's *Die Leiden des jungen Werthers,* is given explicitly and repeatedly in the text. To take a brief example: *"Sous prétexte de liberté et de progrès, la societé avait encore découvert le moyen d'aggraver la misérable condition de l'homme . . ."* ("Under the pretext of freedom and progress, society had yet again found a way to exacerbate the miserable human condition . . ."). He continues:

> *Ah! Si jamais, au nom de la pitié, l'inutile procréation devait être abolie, c'était maintenant! Mais ici, encore, les lois édictées par des Portalis ou des Homais apparaissaient, féroces et étranges.*[20]
> (Oh, if ever for pity's sake there were a time to abolish useless procreation, it was now! But here again, laws decreed by the Portalis and Homais of the world appeared, ferocious and strange.)

Only the self can nourish, but as Frederick Garber has suggested, the "autonomy of the self"[21] reaches its terminus in the work of Huysmans. Beyond it stands Kafka's gaunt hunger artist, paradoxically sustained by an absence of sustenance, devouring the void just as Beckett's characters will do.

Not only, then, do Huysmans's bold attempts to suppress traditional plot and to be new at all costs announce a Modernist agenda, reading like so many of the manifestoes of the early twentieth century; the novel, in its opening up of new, nonmimetic possibilities, simultaneously locks out traditional societal and political possibilities. Appearing as it does some one hundred years after 1789, it remains a century later a vital link in our understanding of the structuring power of postrevolutionary individualism in the context of the novel, the genre of democratic individualism *par excellence*.

Fleeing *égalité*, des Esseintes's only *liberté* is to be found in total claustration. As Françoise Gaillard has pointed out, the linguistic analogue to *égalité* is the liberation and leveling of the signifier.[22] In horror, des Esseintes hermetically recoils in a typically Modernist gesture of enclosed absence. Now when I remarked above, perhaps somewhat cryptically, that the paradox of fictional closure duplicates the mechanism of revolution itself, I meant that whenever an *ancien régime* is overturned—be it political or literary—there is an equal and necessary movement toward reaction. Huysmans's proto-Modernist rejection of teleology, character development and traditional closure leads him to a closure more final than that of any so-called traditional fiction. The Latin *claudere*, after all, can be translated as "to shut in" as well as "to end." As any societal or textual hierarchy is leveled, there seems to be a tendency toward, if not the transcendent, then the univocal, even if the univocal is that of "certain uncertainty," as in the work of Kafka or Beckett.[23]

Whether it be totalitarian politics, religious conversion, hyper-aestheticism or, for that matter, the tyranny of the signifier (and

Modernism has conspicuous, and in some cases ominous, affinities with each of these), there is a relinquishing of societal possibilities, a handing over of power to a transcendent, omnipresent or suprapersonal Other. In this light, Barbey d'Aurevilly's famous comment about *A rebours* (which Huysmans proudly quotes in his "Préface"), that "Après un tel livre, il ne reste plus à l'auteur qu'à choisir entre la bouche d'un pistolet ou les pieds de la croix"[24] ("After such a book the author can only choose between a pistol barrel and the foot of the cross") takes on new significance. The choice is between two versions of a single gesture of resignation.

Notes

1. See especially Ruth Plaut Weinreb, "Structural Techniques in *A Rebours*," *The French Review* 49, no. 2 (1975): 222–33; David Mickelson, "*A Rebours:* Spatial Form," *French Forum* 3 (1978): 48–55; Joseph Halpern, "Decadent Narrative: *A Rebours*," *Stanford French Review* 2 (1978): 91–102; Benoît Neiss, "Huysmans et le problème du moderne," *Revue des sciences humaines* 170–71 (1978): 100–08; Françoise Gaillard, "*A Rebours:* une écriture de la crise," *Revue des sciences humaines* 170–71 (1978): 111–22; Jefferson Humphries, "Flaubert's Parrot and Huysmans's Cricket: The Decadence of Realism and the Realism of Decadence," *Stanford French Review* 11 (1987): 323–30.

2. Simon Schama, *Citizens: A Chronicle of the French Revolution* (New York: Alfred A. Knopf, 1989), 6.

3. See his chapter on Huysmans, "Huysmans et la thébaïde raffinée," 153–74 in *La Prison romantique* (Paris: Corti, 1975).

4. J.-K. Huysmans, *A rebours* (Paris: Gallimard Folio, 1977), édition présentée, établie et annotée par Marc Fumaroli, 55. The translations that follow in the text are my own.

5. Ibid., 58.

6. Ibid., 59.

7. Ibid., 71: "*Il y avait beaucoup de choses que Zola ne pouvait comprendre; d'abord, ce besoin que j'éprouvais d'ouvrir les fenêtres, de fuir un milieu où j'étouffais; puis, le désir qui m'appréhendais de secouer les préjugés, de briser les limites du roman . . . Moi, c'était cela qui me frappait surtout à l'époque, supprimer l'intrigue traditionnelle, voire même la passion, la femme, concentrer le pinceau de lumière sur un seul personnage, faire à tout prix du neuf.*"

8. See especially D. A. Miller's *Narrative and Its Discontents: Problems of Closure in the Traditional Novel* (Princeton: Princeton University Press, 1981).

9. Huysmans, 11.

10. The quotation is from Brombert's own translation, *The Romantic Prison* (Princeton: Princeton University Press, 1978), 160.

11. Huysmans, 86.

12. Ibid., 88.

13. Louis Dumont, *Essays on Individualism* (Chicago: Chicago University Press, 1986), 92.

14. Ibid., 96, no. 40.

15. Huysmans, 173.

16. Ibid., 107.

17. Dumont, 279.

18. Huysmans, 254.

19. Joseph Frank, *The Widening Gyre: Crisis and Mastery in Modern Literature* (Bloomington: Indiana University Press, 1968), 60.

20. Huysmans, 294.

21. See *The Autonomy of the Self from Richardson to Huysmans* (Princeton: Princeton University Press, 1982), 278–95.

22. Gaillard, 120.

23. The expression is Dominique Lehl's, from *"Die bestimmte Unbestimmtheit bei Kafka und Beckett,"* 173–88 in *Franz Kafka: Themen und Probleme,* herausgegeben von Claude David (Göttingen: Vanderhoeck und Ruprecht, 1980).

24. Huysmans, 77.

Decadent Coherence in Huysmans's *A rebours*

ROY JAY NELSON

In their search for a definition of coherence, linguists and text grammarians early turned to the quest for counterexamples, for texts of more than one sentence that illustrate incoherence. Such efforts have generally met with failure.[1] For every series of utterances so concocted, some reader has been able to imagine a set of circumstances under which the supposedly disconnected sentences would conjoin and make sense. In the coherence game, such sets of circumstances are called "frames" or "scripts."[2] Texts which tend to affirm their own coherence, including most novels, are subject to the same logic.

In addition to appearing under a single general title, a novel may suggest that it is coherent in two principal ways: by repetition (in maintaining a constant "discourse topic") and by connexity (the explicit, linear relationship of premises to conclusion or of causes to effects). Even in the presence of both of these phenomena, novels remain potentially incoherent; as van Dijk points out in *Macrostructure*, repetition (or "referential identity") is neither necessary nor sufficient for coherence,[3] and even clearly caused chains of events in fiction can lead unpredictably far afield from a coherent discourse topic.[4]

The idea of chains of events, concatenations of causes and effects, played an important role in Zola's concept of the "experimental novel,"[5] and when Huysmans's *A rebours* appeared in 1884, the master criticized his disciple for the "confusion" which he saw in the work.[6] For although the referential identity seems to him, if anything, too constant (he complains that the protagonist, des Esseintes, is as mad at the beginning as he is at the end), Zola tells Huysmans he regrets the lack of connexity between chapters, is displeased *"que les morceaux soient toujours amenés par une transition pénible d'auteur, que vous nous montriez enfin un peu la lanterne magique, au hasard des verres"* ("that the sections are introduced by means of forced transitions by the author, that you give us a bit of a magic lantern show, with the slides arranged at random"). And, in reply, Huysmans admits incoherence:

26

"La vérité c'est qu'étant donné le sujet, je n'ai pas pu arriver à le faire autrement, en dépit des obligatoires incohérences qu'il amenait"[7] ("The truth is that, given the subject, I couldn't manage to do it otherwise, despite the unavoidable incoherences that introduces"). Indeed, while Huysmans's text appears unified by repetition, and even though cause and effect play a major role, unless readers produce a minimal "script" for the text, it may well appear incoherent.

The consistent and repeated discourse topic is obviously Jean des Esseintes—ultimate scion of a degenerated noble family—who is, as virtually the only "character" in the work, present on its every page. There is an apparently constant narrative voice throughout as well, expressing itself in consistently long sentences, with parallel subordination and a rich and precise vocabulary, given to composing lists, and capable of seeing through des Esseintes's eyes.

As for linear connexity, cause and effect provide it in *A rebours* on two levels. First, they link the elements of the minimal plot. Jean des Esseintes's extreme sensitivity, doubtless of hereditary origins, produces in him a neurotic fear of disorder and an equally neurotic desire to see himself as different from the common horde. These preoccupations drive him to flee Parisian society, taking up a hermitlike existence in a secluded house in Fontenay-aux-Roses. There, living by night and sleeping by day to avoid contact with his servants, and dining according to menus established once every four months, our hero affirms both his order and his difference. But, instead of relieving his neurotic symptoms, this way of living aggravates them and transforms preexisting physical weaknesses into a life-threatening illness of the digestive tract. Therefore, on doctor's orders, des Esseintes must give up the sequestered existence; he prepares at last to return to his dreaded Parisian social life with a prayer on his lips: *"Seigneur, prenez pitié du Chrétien qui doute . . .,"*[8] ("Lord, take pity on the Christian who doubts . . ."). Thus, the plot establishes a simple causal chain. Neuroses of hereditary origin produce an attempted cure, which leads instead to psychosomatic illness and finally to an apparent religious reconversion.

All the rest of the work consists of ill-connected digressions, describing in detail various preoccupations of des Esseintes at Fontenay: decoration of the rooms of his hermitage; his famous "mouth organ," which played rondos on his palate with combinations of *liqueurs*; the tortoise whose carapace he had gilded and bejeweled to enliven the rugs on which it crawled; his paintings and engravings; his collection of Roman and medieval Latin texts; his reflections on religion, morality, and the Church; his bizarre selection of house plants; his nightmares; his modern readings from Dickens to Mallarmé; his collection

of perfumes and makeup; his musings on love and sexuality; his
aborted trip to London. Causality plays its second role on this level,
connecting each of the sixteen chapters to the central plot (each is an
element of the supposed "cure") and creating within each digression
its own interior chain of events. Twelve of the chapters involve caused
movement from physical stimulus to psychological response—illusion, hallucination, dreaming, sexual arousal, religious sentiments,
and what have since come to be called "Proustian" memories. The
other four chapters (3, 6, 12, and 14) lead from texts or ideas to
general conclusions. Thus, like a tree with various branches, the novel
suggests a kind of structural unity. But the problem arises at the end of
each branch, for each chapter leads us to a sort of dead end (one of des
Esseintes's mental states) from which we must leap, at the start of the
next chapter, either back to the central trunk or ahead to the following
digression, in the absence of believable connecting vocabulary. None
of the branches "causes" any of the others. And indeed, the order of
the episodes seems unimportant; they are, as Zola suggested, quite
interchangeable.

The fact that the episodes overwhelm the central plot by their sheer
volume, and that each, at its end, is causally disconnected from the
rest, suggests a *roman à tiroirs*, in which the constant presence of a
single central character is sufficient to guarantee unity. But is des
Esseintes, as he moves in each chapter from stimulus to new mental
state, really the same person?

Although the structural similarity of the chapters encourages readers to believe there are consistent elements in des Esseintes's reactions,
apparent contradictions create a puzzle. The protagonist believes, for
example, in the forces of determinism. He recalls having cynically
encouraged his relatively impecunious friend d'Aigurande to marry a
woman who had her heart set on living in a new cylindrical apartment
building. As des Esseintes had predicted, this situation led "inevitably" to the collapse of the marriage. In another deterministic experi-
ment, he remembers having debauched a poor and parentally abused
adolescent, prepaying several visits to a luxurious house of prostitution for him. Our hero's assumption was that the lad, once addicted to
such expensive sensuality, would steal and eventually kill to pursue the
habit; to his disappointment, however, des Esseintes never found the
young man's name in the newspapers. Still, convinced as he is of the
basic soundness of deterministic principles, he seems to feel that he is
himself above them, that he can conquer the physical and psychological maladies arising in his own blood, tainted by centuries of aristocratic inbreeding. Indeed, what he despises most in others is their

predictability; he scorns the young, as puppets of lust, and the bourgeois, dominated by greed, because their destiny is already inscribed
in their bloated faces. Is his own scrawny countenance any less predic-
tive?

Des Esseintes's attitude about religion involves equal ambivalence.
His Jesuit upbringing is still frequently with him in his meditations,
and he sees in faith the most efficacious consolation for those who
suffer. Yet he also views Christianity as a "superb legend" and a
"magnificent imposture" (p. 113). He appears to alternate between
yearning for the old order, in which God called the shots, and materialistic determinism. The Church, preserver of art and of a mystic
sense of the miraculous (pp. 112–14) might have been, he thinks, the
inspiration for his own *thébaïde raffinée* in Fontenay, in which he flees
the deterministic causal chains at work in his life. His longing for the
otherworldly, in God or in Satan, could be, he realizes, mechanistically
determined by his religious education.

On one concept, however, des Esseintes appears to hold almost
consistent views: For him, the artificial is preferable to the natural.
Two gleaming, new locomotives he has recently seen are far more
exciting and sensually arousing for him than the natural women to
whom he compares them. Then, too, mechanical fish navigate in the
aquarium he has installed between the porthole in his dining room,
constructed to resemble a ship's cabin, and the exterior window of the
house. The only natural elements he permits in his environment are
his tortoise and his houseplants. But the tortoise is disguised, beneath
a gilded, jewel-incrusted shell; unable to adapt to such splendor, it
soon dies, its carapace remaining as a decorative but purely inanimate
object on the floor. As for the plants, des Esseintes selects the most
artificial-looking varieties he can find, which imitate in their leaves and
blossoms the colors of copper and the forms of wrought iron, or
simulate bits of cloth, animal organs, or diseased human skin. So des
Esseintes indeed desires to perceive organic nature around him, but
only so long as the apparently organic is really manufactured (the
mechanical fish), or if the truly organic appears artificial. This ambivalence leads both des Esseintes and the narrative voice to make a
number of contradictory statements, of which two examples will
suffice to reveal the irony at work on the microlevel. After the comparison of feminine beauty to the splendor of the locomotives, our
hero reflects: "... *l'homme a fait, dans son genre, aussi bien que le Dieu
auquel il croit*" (p. 53) ("... man has been as successful, in his way, as
the God in whom he believes"); thus humanity is at once God's equal
and an inferior who can only trust in divine providence. And when des

Esseintes selects his exotic houseplants, the narrative voice evokes as his motivation *"son penchant naturel vers l'artifice,"* (p. 122) ("his natural inclination toward the artificial").

It is such apparent contradictions that raise the question of isotopy. What sort of "script" can readers construct that will allow for a character's belief in materialistic determinism and his search for the marvelous, that can contain a "natural" penchant for the artificial? The answer lies in the ubiquitous paradoxes themselves, for they are the bipolar unifying factor, endowing each chapter of *A rebours* with a particular irony, which is the hallmark of the novel.

The holding of self-contradictory opinions may be called "perversity" (when one always adopts the opinion contrary to that proposed by one's interlocutor, so that one's opinions are, in effect, determined by that which they oppose), or "hypocrisy," or "sacrilege" (in which a belief system must be accepted in order to be fruitfully profaned). While all of these types of irony are evoked in *A rebours*, the clues for scripting in the novel encourage us to read it essentially as sacrilege.[9]

In *A rebours*, religion and religious authors are a major theme, and, in des Esseintes's mind, the very idea of God inspires the notion of a contrary force:

> *En face d'un Dieu omnipotent, se dressait maintenant un rival plein de force, le Démon, et une affreuse grandeur lui semblait devoir résulter d'un crime pratiqué, en pleine église par un croyant s'acharnant, dans une horrible allégresse, dans une joie toute sadique, à blasphémer, à couvrir d'outrages, à abreuver d'opprobre, les choses révérées . . . (pp. 116–17)*

("Opposite an omnipotent God now rose up a powerful rival: the Demon, and a hideous grandeur seemed to him [des Esseintes] to accrue to crimes carried out right in the church by a believer driving himself, with horrible delight and totally sadistic joy, to blaspheme, to bury the sacred things in outrage and drown them in opprobrium . . .").

The presence of serious religious vocabulary ("right in the church by a believer . . . the sacred things . . . in opprobrium") is the requisite guarantee of the efficacity of the blasphemy as well as of the sadistic joy: Without belief there is no sacrilege.

A similar confrontation of opposites is apparent in the two Gustave Moreau paintings of Salomé's dance, which des Esseintes owns and often contemplates. The first sets its scene in a kind of Gothic cathedral, where, in exchange for the head of John the Baptist, Salomé, caparisoned in jewels (not unlike the tortoise), begins the corrupt and lubricious dance that will arouse old Herod. Des Esseintes sees in her figure, as portrayed by Moreau, *"la déité symbolique de l'indestructible Luxure"* (p. 86) ("the symbolic deity of indestructible Lust"). In the second painting, she poses, her jewels undone from the dance; center stage is now occupied by the gleaming head of St. John, which, risen from the platter on which it had been brought, terrifies the *danseuse* with its flaming glance. The artist has portrayed a victory of the forces of nature (Salomé is explicitly associated with the ancient symbolism of the lotus), and a miraculous revenge of spiritual powers. But miracles happen only in art, and des Esseintes, even before the second painting, is more dominated, like Herod, by the dancer than by the saint: *"Tel que le vieux roi, des Esseintes demeurait écrasé, anéanti, pris de vertige, devant cette danseuse . . ."* (p. 89) ("Like the old king, des Esseintes was left crushed, destroyed, overcome with vertigo as he beheld this dancer"). For the true divinity in this text, the force ordained by God, is Nature. As Françoise Gaillard pointed out in her 1978 paper on the unhinging of referentiality in *A rebours*, since the classical age, Nature had indeed taken the place of the miraculous God of the Middle Ages.[10] Thus when des Esseintes sequesters himself, lives by night, and demands that his world be artificial, he is carrying out sacrilegious attacks on what he sees as God's natural order.

Even literature evolves for him like natural vegetation and elicits his reactions on the same grounds. In Balzac, virtues and vices as codified by the Church appear as healthy plants to des Esseintes: *"floraisons normales plantées dans de la naturelle terre"* (p. 183) ("normal flowering plants, planted in natural earth"). Baudelaire, however, had gone farther; he had descended into the depths of the bottomless pit, discovering diseases there, such as *"le tétanos mystique, la fièvre chaude de la luxure, les typhoïdes et les vomitos du crime"* (p. 183) ("mystic tetanus, the hot fever of lust, the typhoids and the yellow fevers of violent crime"). In Baudelaire's discovery and expression of morbid psychology, des Esseintes finds an *"indicible charme"* (p. 185) ("ineffable charm"); such disease may be one of Nature's reactions to anti-natural attacks. Baudelaire found the linguistic way to accomplish the impossible, the way to admire Evil without thereby transforming it to a Good; in *Les Fleurs du Mal*, he retains Evil in the negative charge of morbid vocabulary while creating the sacrilegious paradox by setting it in an admirative context. Likewise, in *A rebours*, the Fontenay hermitage is the sumptuous and illusory décor paradoxically encasing the disease which is des Esseintes.

Professor Gaillard evoked the paradox: *"l'inversion toujours serve du positif qu'elle condamne . . ."*[11] ("inversion ever the servant of the positive value it condemns"). And Per Buvik defined the relationship of the paradox to disease and death in *A rebours:* "According to the decadents," he wrote, "it is the function of great art to disturb the order of nature; but, taken to extremes, such disturbance necessarily threatens life itself. Ironically, des Esseintes's physical condition grows worse in proportion as his aesthetic quest advances."[12] Indeed, just as the tortoise dies beneath the weight of its gem-incrusted shell (which the text compares to a ciborium), so the protagonist himself is dying away in the artificial splendor of his seclusion. For his disease itself is a natural phenomenon, divine order asserting its power, a revenge of Nature against the unnatural inbreeding which produced him, aggravated by the willed artificiality of his style of life. Likewise, des Esseintes prophetically describes his relapses into the religious faith of his youth as symptoms of a disease. *"Eh! je deviens stupide, se dit des Esseintes; la crainte de cette maladie va finir par déterminer la maladie elle-même, si ça continue"* (p. 114) ("Hey! I'm growing stupid," des Esseintes said to himself; 'if things go on like this, the fear of the disease will end up provoking the disease itself' "). Thus religion, disease, and Nature are all one, in the "script" of this novel, and their basic reaction to des Esseintes's artificial assaults upon them is to yield. Our hero seeks to cultivate illusions artificially—to conjure up a sea voyage from the sights and smells of his ship's cabin dining room, or lost loves through the blending of perfumes. Nature cooperates and soon provides him with illusions beyond his wildest dreams: hideous nightmares and frightening visual and auditory hallucinations. As Ruth Antosh demonstrates in her 1986 book on Huysmans, having sought the past, des Esseintes is quickly suffocating in his own memories.[13] Under concerted assaults, Nature simply begins dying away, thus asserting its essential importance through its incipient absence.

In all des Esseintes's pronouncements, from his aesthetic preference for specially bred, artificial-looking plants to his arguments in favor of contraception and abortion rights (pp. 212–13), he heroically defends human reason over what he sees as Nature's way and God's plan. Yet the narrative voice and the text have another message: Artifice cannot defeat Nature. When des Esseintes at last chooses his own life over death, health over illness, and religious faith (apparently) over reason, his action affirms the paradox of sacrilege. Thus, in order to reconstitute the text as a unified whole, readers must uncover a fundamental and ubiquitous irony between protagonist and text, subsumed in the title, *A rebours*. For des Esseintes must be read not only as defeated but as ironically self-defeating; it is in this sense that he reflects true decadence. Only through the discovery and recovery of this irony can readers see the novel as fully coherent. The sacrilegious paradox therefore appears as a principal intention of this text.

In order to recover this intention, this coherence, in *A rebours*, readers must also give assent to the notion that every counterforce is dependent upon its opposite. In particular, readers must themselves harbor enough faith, or superstition, to understand the powers that are at odds in sacrilege. An ancient irony, derived from the human/divine dichotomy and present in the concept of a "rational animal," sacrilege surfaces in force in late nineteenth-century France (Baudelaire, Villiers de l'Isle-Adam, Barbey d'Aurevilly, Jean Lorrain), beginning a current strongly present in the twentieth century. Gide's *L'Immoraliste* is constructed on a similar ironic coherence, and images and structures of profanation recur in Proust. Jean Genet's *Le Balcon* (not unlike Baudelaire's) loves what it hates and serves what it assails. We are apparently still religious enough to respond to sacrilege and to recover its ironic coherence.

Notes

1. Michel Charolles, "Text Connexity, Text Coherence, and Text Interpretation Processing," *Papers in Textlinguistics*, 49, Emel Sözer, ed. (Hamburg: Helmot Buske Verlag, 1985), 1–2.

2. Madeleine G. Randquist, "The Barely Visible Glue: Some Aspects of Textual Conectedness," *Papers in Textlinguistics*, 49: 189–94.

3. Teun A. van Dijk, *Macrostructures: An Interdisciplinary Study of Global Structures in Discourse, Interaction, and Cognition* (Hillsdale, N.J.: Lawrence Erlbaum Associates, 1980), 36.

4. Ibid., 139.

5. Emile Zola, *Le Roman expérimental*, in his *Oeuvres complètes*, X (Paris: Cercle du Livre Précieux, 1968), 1178–81.

6. Letter to Huysmans, in J. K. Huysmans, *Lettres inédites à Emile Zola* (Geneva: Droz, 1953), 106.

7. Ibid., 103. These and all other translations in the text are mine.

8. Joris-Karl Huysmans, *A rebours* (Paris: Fasquelle, 1955), 269. Further references in the text are to this edition.

9. On sacrilege in decadent novels, see Barbara Kitzner Timmons, "Decadent Style: Studies in the French, Italian, and Spanish Novel of the *fin de siècle*," University of Michigan *diss.* 1983, 98–110 et passim.

10. Françoise Gaillard, "*A rebours*, une écriture de la crise," *Revue des Sciences Humaines*, 170–71 (1978), 113.

11. Ibid.

12. "*Selon les décadents, le propre du grand art consiste à perturber l'ordre de la nature; mais poussée à l'extrême, une telle perturbation doit menacer la vie elle-même. Ironiquement l'état de des Esseintes s'aggrave à mesure qu'avance sa quête esthétique.*" Per Buvik, "Manifeste et roman de crise. A propos d'*A rebours*," *Bulletin de la Société J.-K. Huysmans*, 71, Tome XIX (1980), 16–17.

13. Ruth B. Antosh, *Reality and Illusion in the Novels of J.-K. Huysmans* (Amsterdam: Rodopi, 1986), 67–68.

The End of Illusion in *L'Eve future*

JEFFREY WALLEN

> *"But just as two intersecting lines, converging on one side of a point, reappear on the other after their passage through infinity, and just as our image, as we approach a concave mirror, vanishes to infinity only to reappear before our very eyes, so will grace, having likewise traversed the infinite, return to us once more, and so appear most purely in that bodily form that has either no consciousness at all or an infinite one, which is to say, either in the puppet or a god."* Heinrich von Kleist, "On the Puppet Theatre"[1]

Many works of the late nineteenth century share a fascination with the power of artifice. An increasing emphasis on the autonomy of art, concomitant with the spread of industrial techniques of production and reproduction, served to highlight the divergence of the artificial creation from any organic orgin. One of the most influential works of this time, Huysman's *A rebours* (which has been translated into English as *Against Nature*), presents an aesthetic of the artifice. Yet the unfolding of des Esseintes's paradoxical *"penchant naturel vers l'artifice"* proceeds by a series of dis-illusionments, and the book lavishly describes all the aesthetic pleasures which des Esseintes can no longer enjoy. We are presented with an accelerating dialectic between illusion and disillusionment: *"Après les fleurs factices singeant les véritables fleurs, il voulait des fleurs naturelles imitant des fleurs fausses"*[2] ("tired of artificial flowers aping real ones, he wanted some natural flowers that would look like fakes"). Yet as the demands of sustaining an aesthetic illusion that does not simply mirror the increasingly artificial nature of modern life becomes more complex, we are confronted with a chronicle of the revolt of des Esseintes's body against its artificial environment. The celebration of artifice is framed within a narrative gaze that seeks to dissect more than to fabricate illusions, and the physiological breakdown of the body works finally to dispel the confusion between nature and artifice, reality and illusion, which haunts des Esseintes's quest.

Villiers de l'Isle-Adam's *L'Eve future,* published a few years after *A rebours,* also offers a probing exploration of the powers of artifice. Its two main characters are Lord Ewald, an English Lord who is at the verge of suicide after having been entranced by an image of feminine beauty, and Thomas Edison, the American inventor, who creates a series of devices which record, transmit, and reproduce sounds and images. Yet Edison, rather than an ardent enthusiast of all that is captured and re-created through his inventions, is instead a harsh critic of the effects of imitation, copying, and illusion, and the book begins with his typical decadent lament: *"Comme j'arrive tard dans l'Humanité! murmurait-il. Que ne suis-je l'un des premiers-nés de notre espèce!"*[3] ("What a latecomer I am in the ranks of humanity! Why wasn't I one of the first-born of the species?"). Edison yearns to capture the earliest sounds, the voice of God, even all the metaphors of sound which elude the possibility of mechanical reproduction, such as *"le bruit . . . de la Chute de l'Empire romain"*[4] ("the sound . . . of the fall of the Roman Empire"). Although he himself is presented as almost a translation, as a *"vivante reproduction"*[5] ("living reproduction") of earlier figures, he is discontent with modern life precisely insofar as it offers a falling away from, and a bad imitation of, an earlier time.

Both Edison and Ewald, employing the vocabulary of aestheticism, denounce *"la non-correspondance du physique et de l'intellectuel"*[6] ("the non-correspondence of the physical and the intellectual"), and the existence of only a *"rapport fictif"*[7] ("fictional connection") between the appearance and the reality of modern-day woman; their criticism harks back to an earlier age in which an ideal harmony between body and spirit was conceived as possible. Yet their efforts are not centered around the desire for a return to the achievements of the Greeks; instead, Edison responds to Ewald's plea—*"qui m'ôtera cette âme de ce corps!"*[8] ("who will deliver this soul out of this body")—by attempting to create a new, an artificial "Eve." The response to the disjunction between body and soul (in the person of the beloved), in which the beautiful body contains a soul which is only a reflection of the degraded desires of the bourgeois nineteenth century, is to create an artificial body, an exact replica of the appearance of Miss Alicia Clary, the woman with whom Lord Ewald has fallen in love. The bad copy— Miss Clary is herself described as a living incarnation of *"la Vénus Victrix"* ("the Venus victorious")—is to be replaced by the perfect replica. The techniques of artifice will themselves be used to overcome the debasing effects of living in an artificial age; or in Edison's words to Ewald, *"vous êtes un de ces malades que l'on ne peut traiter que par le poison"*[9] ("you are one of those invalids who can only be cured with poison").

Throughout the text, it is precisely this possibility of duplication, of offering us a repeated or second image of what has already been described, which functions to reveal the illusory nature of the initial appearance or impression. Much of the discussion between Ewald and Edison can be characterized by chapter headings such as "Analysis," or "Dissection," and as the construction of the android proceeds, we are constantly presented with "explanations" of all the processes that will produce the illusory impression of life. The second image, the second version, provides a knowledge of artifice which functions to dispel illusion. The most emblematic scenes of dis-illusionment occur when the artificial means by which women maintain power over men are revealed. Most noticeably in the chapters *"Danse Macabre"* and *"Exhumation"* of the fourth book, we are shown first the *appearance* of Evelyn Habal (the archseductress), and then the real physique, stripped of its makeup. The text here offers a pattern for its own interpretation (a pattern which many critics have seized), in which interpretation itself is seen fundamentally as a process of becoming progressively more free from the seductive and attractive powers of (feminine) illusion.

Interpretation, as an unveiling of truth—or as a process of de-mystification which at least reveals the falsity of earlier interpretations—is a central, and often an essential element of criticism. Edison, after he projects for Ewald the second motion picture of Evelyn Habal, now stripped of her artifices (and this text was written a few years *before* Edison invented the movie camera) remarks: *"Mais . . . c'est la même: seulement c'est la vraie. C'est celle qu'il y avait sous la semblance de l'autre."*[10] ("Why . . . it's the same person; simply, *this is the true one*. It is the person who was hiding beneath the appearance of the other.") And he continues, in this chapter which ironically has an epigraph from Baudelaire, *"Je vois que vous ne vous êtes jamais bien sérieusement rendu compte des progrès de l'Art de la toilette dans les temps modernes, mon cher lord!"* ("I see you've never really taken a serious accounting of the improvements in the art of makeup during these modern times, my lord!"). In a parody of Baudelaire's *"Eloge du maquillage"* ("In Praise of Makeup"), we are then presented with an inventory of the hideous implements by which the rotting body was transformed into an appearance of the ideal.

This unveiling of the illusion of beauty is itself, however, a repetition of an earlier moment in text, where Lord Ewald presented Edison with two versions of Alicia's character, first his translation, *"ma traduction"* of Alicia's story of her past, followed by *"les paroles mêmes d'Alicia"* ("the precise words of Alicia"). Ewald declares, *"je vois bien qu'il me faut vous avouer le* texte *même"* ("and I see clearly that I must set before you the *text* itself"),[11] and then states, *"Voici donc,* exactement, *ses paroles*" ("Here, then, are her *exact* words"). The words that he goes on to offer, however, are not her exact words at all, but a recounting of her activities in indirect discourse, placed within quotation marks. For both Ewald and Edison, the retelling of their disillusionment with women initiates them into the project of creating a new, artificial Eve. Yet the repetition of their own stories, and the comparison of one version against another in which neither "*le* texte *même*" ("the *text* itself") nor the true image (but only its mechanical projection) is presented, suggests that interpretation occurs only as translation, proceeding from the discord between one image, or one text, and another. The duplications, reflections, and repetitions of the text serve less to highlight the difference between a first and a second reading, than to emphasize that reading is the awareness of difference; the second version, rather than leading from appearance to reality, serves to display the "*rapport fictif*" ("fictional connection") which structures every interpretation of the text.

In the case of the two "visions" of Evelyn Habal, however, both images are the projections of a machine which Villiers describes with great care:

> A long strip of transparent plastic encrusted with bits of tinted glass moved laterally along two steel tracks before the luminous cone of the astral lamp. Drawn by a clockwork mechanism at one of its ends, this strip began to glide swiftly between the lens and the disk of a powerful reflector.[12]

The process of interpretation, whether considered as dis-illusionment or as translation, is itself only another effect of the text, generated by the text's machinery. The machines of the text, and most notably, of course, the android, are projectors or transmitters of meanings with which they can never fully coincide. Rodolphe Gasché, attempting to establish, in his words, "the minimal structure that would account for such a diversity of possible, yet ultimately not legitimitizable interpretations," describes *L'Eve future* as a "machine of reading." He writes:

> Not unlike the android that Villiers characterizes as a "machine of visions," *L'Eve future* itself will appear as a machine of reading, of interpretative totalizations. It contains a number of "novels" in the same way that the android is said to contain a number of women. These "novels" are those of the critics, and coincide with their idealizing interpretations of *L'Eve future*. . . . Yet they cannot ultimately be justified since the narrational undecidability of *L'Eve future* makes all these interpretations plausible and simultaneously invalidates them as fixed determinations of its meaning.[13]

The "machine of reading," precisely insofar as it itself is not governed by the imperative to interpret, to find meaning, produces but does not coincide with these "idealizing totalizations." In Gasché's analysis, the artifice does not function as illusion, or as that which reveals illusion; it serves rather to destabilize the categories from which such determinations can be made.

The consideration of the text as machine is common in contemporary critical discourse, and is part of an attempt to move beyond a model of interpretation that is governed by the consciousness of a subject. More broadly, this perspective works to displace an entire set of oppositions—including the real and the illusory, the natural and the artificial—around which interpretation has habitually been based. Paul de Man, for example, in an essay on Rousseau's *Confessions*, contrasts the "text as machine" with the more traditional reading of "text as body":

> Barely concealed by its peripheral function, the text here stages the textual machine of its own constitution *and* performance, its own textual allegory. The threatening element in these incidents then becomes more apparent. The text as body, with all its implications of substitutive tropes ultimately always retraceable to metaphor, is displaced by the text as machine and, in the process, it suffers the loss of the illusion of meaning. The deconstruction of the figural dimension is a process that takes place independently of any desire; as such it is not unconscious but mechanical, systematic in its performance but arbitrary in its principle, like a grammar. This threatens the autobiographical subject not as the loss of something that once was present and that it once possessed, but as the radical estrangement between the meaning and the performance of any text.[14]

De Man's project, of course, is not simply to substitute or to deconstruct the "text as body" with the "text as machine," but rather to analyze the irresolvable process of deciding between or reconciling these two different modes of reading. Nevertheless, it is the "text as machine" which inflicts "the loss of the illusion of meaning," and de Man's readings achieve their "radical estrangement" through an ardent deconstruction which in turn is shown only to differ from, but not to destroy or do away with, the "text as body." But what happens when the machine is indistinguishable from the body? Can we then any longer tell the difference, in *L'Eve future*, between the moment of interpretation which reads the text as body, and the moment which reads the text as machine? When the machine becomes the body, can we be sure that "the loss of the illusion of meaning" is not instead the "illusion of the loss of meaning?" In the next few pages, I will try to sketch out a few preliminary responses to these questions.

The critical endpoint of "undecidability" leaves largely intact the series of differences which it engages and exploits, even as it empties them of any transcendental claim to meaning. In *L'Eve future*, marks of difference are not effaced, but destabilized. The machine is often juxtaposed to the body insofar as it represents the impossibility of embodiment; there is no consciousness, no soul, no meaning interior to the machine. In *L'Eve future*, however, the machine is an android, a simulacrum; it is unclear whether it embodies anything, or what it is that it might embody. The future Eve might be "inhabited" by Sowana, by Mistress Anderson, by the words recorded on her golden lungs, by Edison, by the reflection of Lord Ewald's projected desires, or by an alien spirit. Or, she might even be, as Ewald first imagines in the climactic scene of the book, Alicia Clary herself transformed, finally awakened to a higher spiritual plane of life. In order to decide between these possibilities, it would be necessary to know where the voice originates from, how it is transmitted, and what its relation is to the body that speaks it. Edison's inventions have not only made it impossible to definitively answer these questions, but have made it no longer possible to be sure of the difference between these alternatives. The simulacrum haunts every body and every voice, making unreliable the smooth functioning of any oppositional or differential schema.

The one mark of difference, however, that seemingly continues to operate most strongly in this text is that of sexual difference. In this highly misogynistic book, we are presented only with a female android, and all of the problematics of the body and of incarnation are exclusively mapped out on the female body. As Naomi Schor writes, "Villiers' futuristic fantasy of a female android is the logical conclusion of a century of fetishization of the female body."[15] Is it therefore the operation of sexual difference in the text which must be analyzed and attacked, or rather should the text be critiqued from the ground of sexual difference? Does the substitutability of body and machine provide the avenue for a rethinking of sexual difference, or is the entire simulacral logic of the text itself founded on an attempted repression of sexual difference? The creation of the female android puts into question the nature of sexual difference; her "sex" cannot be determined. It is suggested that Ewald will not have sexual intercourse with the android Hadaly, and that she is sterile; Edison makes no attempt to create a fertile womb for her (in contrast, for example, to the "new Eve" created in Angela Carter's *The Passion of New Eve*). Yet this de-gendering and sterilization of the female figure is certainly another mark of the misogyny of the text. The instauration of the simulacrum also undermines the operation of sexual difference, but there is no guarantee that a shift from creation to invention, from illusion to simulacrum, from embodiment to replication will in any way work to overcome forces of domination and subjection which are grounded in sexual difference; one might certainly argue conversely that losing the ability to "tell the difference" will lead instead to a freer reign of these forces. Sexual difference both resists and instigates the entire problematic of difference in *L'Eve future*, but it cannot finally determine its outcome. The work of the critic is itself only a simulacralization, rather than a sacralization, of the text—another re-duplication, transmission, and re-engendering which does not arrive at either the ground or the abyss of knowledge—and it is therefore precisely this challenge of re-figuring the future of *L'Eve future* which confronts the critic.

Notes

1. Heinrich von Kleist, "On the Puppet Theatre," *An Abyss Deep Enough,* translated by Philip B. Miller, (New York, 1982), 216.
2. Joris-Karl Huysmans, *A rebours,* (Paris, 1977), 191. English translation by Robert Baldick, *Against Nature,* (Harmondsworth, Middlesex, 1959), 97.
3. Villiers de l'Isle-Adam, *L'Eve future,* (Paris, 1960), 15. English translation by Robert Martin Adams, *Tomorrow's Eve,* (Urbana, 1982), 9. Subsequent references to the English translation will appear in parentheses following the French citation. I will translate directly citations of only a few words.
4. Ibid., 18 (10).
5. Ibid., 12.
6. Ibid., 65.
7. Ibid., 61.
8. Ibid., 80 (44).
9. Ibid., 89 (49).
10. Ibid., 204 (118). Emphasis in the original.
11. Ibid., 59 (33). Emphasis in the original.
12. *"Une longue lame d'étoffe gommée, incrustée d'une multitude des verres exigus, aux transparences teintées, se tendit latéralement entre deux tiges d'acier devant le foyer lumineux de la lampe astrale. Cette lame d'étoffe, tirée à l'un des bouts par un mouvement d'horloge, commença de glisser, très vivement, entre la lentille et le timbre d'un puissant réflecteur."* Ibid., 201 (117).
13. Rodolphe Gasché, "The Stelliferous Fold: On Villiers de l'Isle-Adam's *L'Eve future,*" *Studies in Romanticism* 22 (Summer 1983): 300–01.
14. Paul de Man, *Allegories of Reading,* (New Haven, 1979), 298.
15. Naomi Schor, *Breaking the Chain,* (New York, 1985), 146.

Fin-de-siècle Télétechnè: Villiers de l'Isle-Adam and Jules Verne

FRANC SCHUEREWEGEN

Have a gramophone in every grave or keep it in the house. After dinner on a Sunday. Put on poor old greatgrandfather. Kraahraark! Hellohellohello amawfullyglad kraark awfullygladaseeagain hellohello amawf krpthsth.
James Joyce, Ulysses, II.

In a recent text, Jean-François Lyotard writes: *"La question qui nous est posée par les technologies nouvelles quant à leur rapport avec l'art, est celle de l'ici et maintenant"* ("The question that the new technologies ask us, in regard to their relation to art, concerns the here and now").[1] By this he means to suggest that the important technoscientific development of our era has resulted, in the aesthetic domain (and probably elsewhere), in a *"désancrage"* ("uprootedness") and a *"délocalisation"* ("dislocation"). Thus, today, the individual at grips with technology finds it harder and harder to take his or her bearings in immediate time and space, in the *hic et nunc* of his or her existence. *"L'idée même qu'il y a une réception 'initiale,' ce qu'on appelle depuis Kant une 'esthétique,' un mode, empirique ou transcendental d'affection de l'esprit par une 'matière' (. . .) qui lui arrive ici et maintenant, cette idée paraît d'un archaïsme désuet"* ("The very idea that there is an 'initial' reception—which since Kant we have called an 'aesthetic,' an empirical or transcendental mode of affection of the spirit by 'matter' (. . .) that occurs here and now—seems archaic and obsolete").[2]

The effects noted by Lyotard are particularly apparent in the field of "telecommunications." Now that science can bring into contact categories of time and space that we had previously learned to regard as incompatible, the categories of *déixis*—which organize our perception of reality and externalize it in language—have been seriously affected. *"Que désigne 'ici' quand on est au téléphone, à la télévision, au récepteur du téléscope électronique? Et le maintenant? Est-ce que la compo-*

Translations by Ann Willeford.

sante 'télé' ne brouille pas nécessairement la présence, l' "ici-maintenant" des formes et de leur réception 'charnelle'?" ("What does 'here' mean when one is on the telephone, on television, or looking into an electronic telescope? And the 'now'? Doesn't the prefix 'tele' necessarily obfuscate the presence, the 'here-and-now' of forms and of their 'physical' reception?")[3]

1. Roused to indignation by the telephone

In the first book of Villiers de l'Isle-Adam's *L'Eve future*, we see Edison (i.e., the character bearing that name) use a phonograph to dictate into a telephone a message that the *"grand électricien"* ("great electrician") does not deign to articulate himself. *"Oui, c'est moi, Monsieur Edison"* ("Yes, it is I, Mr. Edison"), announces *"une voix forte"* ("a loud voice") of whose owner or origin we are unaware.[4] The scene is repeated further on in the second book. This time, the engineer must *"donner vivement une tape au phonographe"* ("hit the phonograph hard") (p. 846) to make the machine agree to speak in his place. . . .

Villiers, who never missed a chance to attack positivism and the cult of Progress, is attacking here the instruments for reproducing and recording the voice which arrived in France in 1878.[5] But there is more at stake in these pages than merely willful derision on the part of an author whom *"le téléphone et le phonographe avaient positivement indigné"* ("the telephone and the phonograph had positively roused to indignation").[6] By putting a telecommunications screen between himself and the "outside," the "hero" (p. 765) of *L'Eve future* also involves himself in a philosophical and aesthetic debate.

Critics have often called attention to the ambivalent character of Villiers's attitude. Despite his prejudice against positivism, the author is obviously attracted *"par le côté spectaculaire de la réalisation scientifique"* ("by the spectacular side of scientific achievement").[7] This *"attirance troublée"* ("ambivalent attraction"), this *"répugnance intéressée"* ("interested revulsion")[8] add a considerable nuance to the received image we have of Villiers as hero of the antitechnological struggle. But from my perspective it is especially important to establish a link between the author's hesitancy in regard to science and the *type* of technology represented by Edison in *L'Eve future*. For if the instruments for the long-distance transmission of information hold an indisputable fascination for Villiers, it is also true that they impose on their user the experience of "dislocation" and "uprooting" that Lyotard, in our own *fin de siècle*, holds responsible for *"[une] crise profonde de l'esthétique et (. . .) des arts,"* (a "profound crisis in aesthetics and the arts").[9] I would like to suggest that Villiers's story, an early science-fiction novel, anticipates the conclusions of the philosopher by almost a century. And this reading is supported whether the "sorcerer of Menlo Park" behaves as an aesthete or as a scientist, or even if we regard him as an artist disguised as a man of science.[10] What *télétechnè* in *L'Eve future* allows us to question is the relation between *aisthêsis* and presence.

2. His master's voice

In Villiers's work, Edison's most spectacular invention—the one that becomes the emblem of the "great inventor"—is the phonograph. A "magical" object that allows us to break through the limits of both time and space (a capacity that makes the phonograph even more impressive than the telephone), this machine for recording and re-producing the voice is, for Villiers, one of the most powerful "disloca-tion" devices imaginable.

It is the phonograph that allows Edison to *"ravir la présence"* ("steal the presence") of a being (p. 835) by capturing its voice, the voice being the closest thing to its soul, and, hence, to its "essence." (As we shall see, one finds a similar theft in Jules Verne's work.) It is also this machine that is particular to the "Human Imitation" (p. 832) con-structed by the engineer, itself unprecedented in tradition. *"Ce qui donne à l'Andréide son indispensable nouveauté"* notes Jacques Noiray, *"ce qui la distingue des automates imparfaits qui l'ont précédée, ce n'est pas tant l'usage de l'électricité que la maîtrise du langage"* ("What gives the Android its indispensable novelty, what distinguishes her from the imperfect automata preceding her, is not so much the use of electricity as it is the mastery of language").[11] And it is true that it is insofar as she is a machine capable of speech, or, if you like, insofar as she is a *walking phonograph*, that Hadaly—or the "Android"—succeeds in creating an illusion, that is to say, in seducing Lord Ewald in such a way that he becomes completely infatuated with her.

Consequently, it is not an exaggeration to say that, despite his anti-positivism, Villiers *needs* the phonograph, and the vast philosophical-aesthetic inquiry that the novel proposes to us would have been unthinkable if the engineer's invention had not preceded it. An object of derision, the target of anti-technological hatred, the phonograph is also, paradoxically, a *condition of possibility*. As Jacques Noiray writes, *"C'est seulement à partir du moment où la science 'permet aux machines de prendre la parole' que peut se déclencher le processus d'idéalisation qui*

donne à la tentative de lord Ewald et d'Edison sa signification métaphysi-
que profonde" ("Only when science 'allows machines to speak' can the
process of idealization be triggered—and it is this process that gives
Lord Ewald's and Edison's endeavor its profound metaphysical significance").[12]

It becomes clear that the phonograph is more than an object of
mockery, that one can even consider it as a possible "source" of the
"message" that *L'Eve future* may illustrate, when we consider that
Villiers's idealism (to which Jacques Noiray alludes when he evokes
the "process of idealization" in the novel) is, above all, an "illu-
sionism." It is well-known that Villiers is convinced not only that *"nos*
sens nous dupent" ("our senses deceive us"), but also that *"nous sommes*
libres de nous créer une vérité personnelle en choisissant ce que nous
préférons considérer comme réel" ("We are free to create a personal truth
for ourselves by choosing what we prefer to consider as real").[13]
"(. . .) il n'est, pour l'Homme, d'autre vérité que celle qu'il accepte de
croire entre toutes les autres,—aussi douteuses que celle qu'il choisit" ("For
Man, there is no other truth than the one he decides to believe among
all others—all of which are as doubtful as the one he chooses"),
explains the Android to Lord Ewald, and she adds: *"Choisis donc celle*
qui te rend un dieu" ("Choose therefore the one that makes you a god")
(p. 991). Such a doctrine, derived by Villiers from his occasionally
hasty readings of Hegel and Schopenhauer, also can be better understood when placed in the context of the phenomenon of "teletechnology."

Let us recall the pages in which Edison explains to Lord Ewald how
to communicate with the Android. This "communication" is far from
obvious. Like a parrot, Hadaly tirelessly repeats the same sentences
engraved upon the two gold cylinders lodged in her chest. When Lord
Ewald inquires whether mere repetition doesn't risk becoming boring,
Edison replies, *"Entre deux êtres qui s'aiment toute nouveauté d'aspect ne*
peut qu'entraîner la diminution du prestige, altérer la passion, faire envoler
le rêve" ("For two people in love, any change in the other's appearance
will inevitably result in a loss of prestige, the diminution of passion,
and the disappearance of the dream") (p. 915). Love is always accom-
panied by a certain "monotony" without which one could not make
the illusion last or put off the always-disappointing encounter with
reality. Edison defines "the great monotonous hour" in these terms:

> *Eterniser une seule heure de l'amour,—la plus belle,—celle, par exemple, où le*
> *mutuel aveu se perdit sous l'éclair du premier baiser, oh! l'arrêter au passage, la*
> *fixer et s'y définir! y incarner son esprit et son dernier voeu! ne serait-ce donc*
> *point le rêve de tous les êtres humains?* (p. 917)

(To eternalize a single hour of love—the most beautiful—the one, for example, when mutual avowal was eclipsed by the lightning of the first kiss, oh! to stop it in flight, to immobilize it and define oneself in it! to embody in it one's spirit, and one's last wish! would not this be the dream of all human beings?)

Thus, what had initially presented itself as one of the numerous instances of Villiers's mockery now suddenly becomes serious. And the reader may well wonder if the conception of alterity he sees defended here (an "idealist" conception which seems to be the direct result of the anti-positivist jokes accumulated at the beginning of the book) is not simply the *effect* on Villiers's thought of a certain state of technological advancement. To immobilize communication, to block it at a pre-dialogical stage (that instant in which the other speaks to me, but before I am obliged to answer him or her), to empty it of duration, to reproduce infinitely this "ideal hour" (p. 917) where everything is possible and nothing happens . . . are we not dealing here with a veritable *phonographic fantasy*?

3. A troglodyte's prejudice

It is therefore permissible to think that "the theory of beauty" presented in *L'Eve future* owes its existence, first and foremost, and even if Villiers suggests the contrary, to science, i.e., to the very thing against which the author claims to be protesting. What the novel proposes to formulate, in a half-mocking, half-"philosophical" vocabulary which hides and reveals at the same time the origin of the phenomenon in question, is an experience of off-centering and non-presence of self, very probably due to a sort of cultural shock between "neotechnical" man[14] and the objects he is capable of producing.

It is noteworthy, moreover, that Villiers reveals his need for technology through the very same means he uses to deny this "need." We must recall here one of Edison's remarks as he explains to Lord Ewald how the Android works. *"Se ressembler! Quel est ce préjugé des temps lacustres, ou troglodytes!"* ("To resemble one another! What is this prejudice of lacustrian, or troglodyte times!") (p. 838) cries the great engineer to his interlocutor who wants to know if Edison can reproduce "the identity" of a woman. If the scientist rejects the idea of resemblance, it is because he has also abandoned the notion of identity, because he refuses to distinguish between copy and model, between the false and the true. . . . Villiers, it seems, cannot accept such a radical position, even if it is completely within the logic of his "hero's" plan. As if he had been carried away by a theme he does not completely "control," the author decides, rather abruptly in fact—since the trace of this about-face is still visible in the text—to "de-technologize" his novel and to dissociate himself from a character whom the reader may have considered, ever so briefly, to be his spokesman.

In the last pages of the novel, the Android escapes from Edison. She becomes the "property," so to speak, of "Sowana," a mysterious "clairvoyant" who manages to "incorporate herself" (p. 1006) into the machine and who, from that moment on, commands it. This transfer of powers might initially seem to be the replacement of one form of remote control by another—seated at a *"clavier d'induction"* ("control panel"), Sowana maintains *"un courant entre elle et l'Andréïde"* ("a current between herself and the Android") (p. 1008)—but it is in fact a gesture of identification—and unification. That is to say, Sowana *becomes* Hadaly, or, rather, a composite being is created, Sowana/Hadaly, who takes the place of the robot.

Ross Chambers has called attention to the hesitancy inscribed in the final pages of *L'Eve future*, a novel organized, at least up to a certain point, according to the model of the "fantastic" described by Todorov. *"Etre d'outre-monde"* ("being from another world") (p. 1010) or mere machine, angel or automaton. What, finally, is Hadaly's status, what does she represent? *"Rien ne peut être tranché"* ("Nothing can be decided definitively"), concludes Chambers, *"et le livre entretient entre l'occultisme et le subjectivisme une savante équivoque où l'on peut reconnaître l'ambiguïté d'une bonne partie de la pensée symboliste"* ("and the book maintains a skillful ambiguity between occultism and subjectivism in which one can recognize the ambiguity of a good part of symbolist thought").[15] But we must also admit that the final pages of the novel are marked by a much more "canonical" idealism than what is found earlier. Villiers again places under the aegis of Hegel and Plato a novel that, in its opening chapters, sometimes seems close to what Nietzsche was propounding more or less in the same era. Thus a legitimate question arises: If Edison's enterprise consists in striking down the edifice of metaphysics, is it not somehow Sowana's role to repair the damage? Doesn't the clairvoyant teach us that, behind "reality", there is "the Real", that is to say, the world "of ideas"? Thus, if one will only believe in this ideal world, it will, despite everything—despite what Edison has suggested—provide a foundation for our existence.[16]

Let us conclude, then, that there is probably a good measure of repression in Villiers's troubled fascination with science, in general, and "telecommunication," in particular. Seduced by the possibilities offered by Edison's inventions, taking inspiration, perhaps, from the workings of these devices through the perfection of a doctrine recommending voluntary confinement in illusion, Villiers also seems panic-stricken at the consequences of his fascination. Thus, the only thing he can do is turn back. The "philosophical" triumphs over fiction, the thesis, over the novel. Villiers seems incapable of following his intuitions to their logical conclusions. . . .

4. Perversity of the phonograph

Such is not the case for Jules Verne, to whom I will devote the last part of this study. In *Le Château des Carpathes* (1892), published six years after the publication in volume form of *L'Eve future*, Verne seems simultaneously to pick up the teletechnic thematic touched upon by Villiers (in fact, Verne is directly inspired by his predecessor's book[17]) and to "harden" it—that is, to radicalize the "perverse" impact of teletechnology on the human being. For the paradox of anti-positivism that we see in the work of Villiers (who condemns in the techno-scientific paradigm the very basis of his own reasoning), *Le Château des Carpathes* substitutes something like a *scientistic paradox*. The proponent of the *"positif et pratique XIXe siècle"* ("positive and practical nineteenth century"), as Verne describes his era in the foreword to the novel[18], does not hesitate here to present an extremely somber vision of scientific progress and telecommunication. Verne's pessimism can be explained by the relation between the man and his work,[19] but also by the "nature" of the science in question. For "teletechnology" appears here again as a force that disturbs, that disarranges, and that jumbles points of reference. . . .

Le Château des Carpathes tells the story of Rodolphe de Gortz, who, with the help of his companion Orfanik, an unrecognized inventor, succeeds in resuscitating a dead singer, "La Stilla," by using a clever arrangement of mirrors and a phonograph containing the voice of the deceased artist. Rather curiously, there is no significant difference between Gortz's attitude as he contemplates La Stilla on stage at the opera, and the behavior of the baron when later, alone in his castle, he abandons himself to the delights of a "sound and light" show. It is as if the death of the singer could not really affect Baron de Gortz, as if, on the contrary, the disappearance of La Stilla even intensified the aesthetic pleasure of the "dilettante."

At this point the reader starts to wonder: "What if La Stilla had never "existed"? What if there had been only from the very beginning, this sort of sound-and-light doll that some believed to be a real woman? This hypothesis is even more plausible in that it corresponds to the very same discovery, made to his own detriment, by Franz de Telek, who is the rival and as we also realize later, the double of Rodolphe de Gortz. Having fallen in love with the actress, and believing he sees a woman behind the artist, he wants to "save" this woman from the theater (p. 148). In this way, Count Telek is directly responsible for the "death" of the diva. But this "death" is suspect. Can La Stilla really "die"? Doesn't the narrative continuously resuscitate her? Isn't what we are initially tempted to see as *une mise à mort* (a killing) really *une mise en évidence* (a revelation), an interval that permits the novelist to reaffirm the fictive nature of his character?

What follows confirms this reading. After several vicissitudes, in the course of which the young count succumbs a second time to the referential illusion (Franz mistakes for a woman the "projection" of La Stilla on the tower of the château des Carpathes), de Telek (whose name is of course symbolic) finally accepts the obvious. His plan to marry the singer and to rescue her from the theater was condemned from the start. It is impossible to look at La Stilla in any other way than how Gortz does. That is why, in the last pages of the narrative, the count ends up taking the place of the baron, who has disappeared. Having inherited the phonographs on which Orfanik has recorded the repertory of La Stilla, Franz de Telek will henceforth be alone in observing the cult of the dead-yet-alive singer.

5. History repeats itself

It is clear that the aesthetic or aesthetic-amorous pleasure that derives in Verne's narrative from listening to the phonograph relies, as it does in *L'Eve future*, upon a deliberate elimination of alterity as presence. But Verne goes farther than Villiers in focusing the attention of the Gortz/de Telek couple, not on a moment of emergence (I refuse to let the other approach by repeating indefinitely the moment of his "approach"), but on a phenomenon of evanescence (I delight in the repetition of the "death" of the other). I am thinking here of the box (p. 232) containing the swan song of La Stilla, the delight of the Baron de Gortz before a bullet destroys it. More generally, in *Le Château des Carpathes*, to listen to the phonograph is to be present at a killing; it is to rejoice in this moment that the intervention of the machine makes infinitely reproducible, in which the facsimile is substituted for the original.

Now, what is distinctive about La Stilla as a character is the fact that she represents in the text nothing more than the possibility of such a substitution. La Stilla does not really exist; the experience of Franz de

Telek is there to demonstrate that to us. She appears in the book only in order to indicate the precariousness of the category of "existence" in a universe governed by the laws of telecommunication. In contrast to Villiers who, despite his hesitancy, eventually reintroduces a clear distinction between copy and model, between false and true (even if it be from an idealistic perspective where what is declared "true" is in fact an undecidable), Verne seems to want to eliminate the original, to deny its existence. Where *télétechnè* rules, reality can slip at any moment into representation, and vice versa. There is no longer any "ontological" certainty.

"*Ce que Jules Verne pressent dans* Le Château des Carpathes" writes Max Milner, "*c'est que les techniques audiovisuelles ne sont pas seulement des prothèses qui s'ajoutent aux autres instruments dont l'homme dispose pour transformer le monde, mais qu'elles ouvrent, dans la réalité opaque et compacte qui nous entoure, des brèches où s'engouffrent notre passion de l'irréel et notre compulsion de répétition, qui est une des manifestations de l'instinct de mort*"

("What Jules Verne foresees in *Le Château des Carpathes* is that audiovisual techniques [Lyotard would doubtless speak here of *télétechnè*] are not only prosthetic devices along with other instruments that enable man to transform the world; they also create, in the opaque and compact reality that surrounds us, openings into which surge our passion for the unreal and our compulsion for repetition, which is one of the manifestations of the death instinct").[20]

To this perceptive observation, we might add that the "repetition compulsion" in Max Milner's term is not only an element of the novel's content but also of its *form*. A story of repetition, of the return of the same in the other, *Le Château des Carpathes* is also a story *which repeats itself* and which manages, in the arrangement of its closure, to prolong the repetition beyond the end of the text. As others have already noted, everything is double in this novel.[21] Moreover, when the narrator observes, in the last lines of the book, that the château des Carpathes is still there, a little more dilapidated than before, certainly, but still "present" as a fantastical entity, or when Verne notes that, despite the demystification we have observed, the populace of Werst is as superstitious as before, is not everything in place so that the story can, in effect, *begin again,* so that another de Gortz or another de Telek can set forth anew on the same path trod by their predecessors?

We could almost say that there is something "phonographic" in Verne's very writing. It is a writing of repetition and return which, despite its false transparence, despite its apparent "readability," applies the "repetition compulsion" to itself, the "mark" of the two protagonists perverted by teletechnology. Thus, *Le Château des Carpathes* is perhaps the missing link between the slightly embarrassed technologism of Villiers, who foresees the perversion inherent in the teletechnical phenomenon but believes he can correct it by a metaphysical point of view, and the place that *télétechnè* will hold in twentieth-century literature. Verne goes farther than Villiers, probably because his essentially favorable attitude towards science makes him more "lucid" in regard to this new paradigm which so completely confuses the relation between man and reality. But the author of *Le Château des Carpathes* is not a modernist like Kafka or Joyce, who, writing from a "telegramophonic"[22] distance, will make that distance the principle of their writing.

I would also point out, at the risk of contradicting myself, that if Jules Verne, in *Le Château des Carpathes*, opts for a writing of repetition, thereby "confirming," on the level of the narrative signifier, the two protagonists' belief that is is possible to stop time, to eliminate duration (like a phonograph, the Vernien narrative "retells" the same fantasy a certain number of times, that of a death eternally postponed), the author also shows that he is indeed "of his time." For this novel of 1892, despite its "science-fiction" character, is also marked by the *fin-de-siècle* spirit, the feeling, sometimes called "decadent," that one is living the end of history, that everything has been done and that nothing new is possible. *"Nous sommes d'un temps où tout arrive,"* writes Verne in the prefatory text, and he corrects himself immediately: *"On a presque le droit de dire où tout est arrivé"* ("We are of a time when everything happens . . . one can almost say, in which everything has happened") (p. 2). This is a significant rectification which denies, strangely, at the beginning of the narrative, the possibility of a historical dynamic, and which allows us from then on to compare Verne's text with the writings, from the same period, of a Huysmans, a Schwob, or a Jean Lorrain. . . . But this sentence also reveals immediately why it is that Verne, after Villiers, and following the latter's "example," placed the narrative of *Le Château des Carpathes* under the protection of Edison and, in particular, of the phonograph. The machine for reproducing the voice succeeds in its fashion in *immobilizing* history, in safeguarding its reproducibility—the future, here, being nothing more than the mechanical repetition of a past, or, rather, of the past that the subject "chooses" to repeat.

A history of the phonograph, Verne's story also leads us to something like a *phonographic conception of history*. That the end of our own century, as has been suggested, has become the echo of the readings presented here, is perhaps merely the *a posteriori* confirmation of Verne's thesis. The phonograph, it seems, has not stopped turning.

The scenario that "postmodern" man (I use the word in the sense given it by Lyotard) is in the process of living is one of "dislocation" and "uprooting" which dates at the least from the end of the last century.

Notes

1. *"Quelque chose comme: 'communication . . . sans communication'"*, in *L'inhumain. Causeries sur le temps* (Paris: Galilée, 1988), 129.

2. *"Logos et tekhnè, ou la télégraphie,"* Ibid., 60.

3. "Quelque chose comme . . .", 128.

4. *L'Eve future*, in Villiers de l'Isle-Adam, *Oeuvres complètes*, vol. 1, A. Raitt and P.-G. Castex, eds. (Paris: Gallimard, Bibliothèque de la Pléïade, 1986), 778. All subsequent references to Villiers will be incorporated into the text.

5. See Jacques Noiray, *Le Romancier et la machine. L'Image de la machine dans le roman français (1850–1900)* (Paris: Corti, 1982), Vol. II, 281 ff.

6. This was the comment of a contemporary: Henri Laujol, *Revue bleue*, 21 Sept. 1889, in Noiray, 244.

7. A. W. Raitt, *Villiers de l'Isle-Adam et le mouvement symboliste* (Paris: Corti, 1982), 178–79.

8. Noiray, 263.

9. "Logos . . .," 60.

10. Edison *"représente l'homme de science idéal selon Villiers: savant rigoureux en même temps qu'artiste"* ("represents the ideal man of science according to Villiers: a rigorous scientist who is also an artist"). Sylain Matton, "Le jeu de la technique et de l'imaginaire dans *L'Eve future* de Villiers de l'Isle-Adam," *Les études philosophiques* (1985): 52.

11. *Le romancier et la machine*, Vol. II, 284.

12. Ibid.

13. Raitt, 248.

14. I have borrowed this expression from J. Noiray, op. cit., Vol. I, 15.

15. *L'Ange et l'automate. Variations sur le mythe de l'actrice* (Paris: Minard, Archives des lettres modernes, 1971), 50.

16. On the Symbolist "faith," see D. Conyngham, *Le Silence éloquent. Thèmes et structures de l'Eve future de Villiers de l'Isle-Adam* (Paris: Corti, 1975), Ch. II. See also Ch. Berg, "Le dîner de têtes," *Revue de l'Université de Bruxelles*, 3 (1981): 9–10.

17. See M. Moré, *Nouvelles Explorations sur Jules Verne* (Paris: Gallimard, 1963), 197 ff.

18. *Le Château des Carpathes* (Paris: Livre de poche, 1987), 2. Subsequent references will be noted in the text.

19. See Simone Vierne, *Jules Verne* (Paris: Balland, 1986), 87 ff.

20. *La Fantasmagorie* (Paris: P.U.F., 1982), 223.

21. See Vierne, 337 ff. See also Luc Rasson, *Châteaux littéraires*, forthcoming.

22. Jacques Derrida, *Ulysse gramophone. Deux mots pour Joyce* (Paris: Galilée, 1987), p. 90. See also my book: *Réelles distances* forthcoming (Presses de l'Université de Lille).

Rachilde: *Fin-de-siècle* Perspective on Perversities

WILL L. McLENDON

So far from constituting a threat to "good" moral values of the *belle époque*, the offbeat French novel of the 1880s and 1890s, often subtitled "Parisian Manners" or even "Foreign Manners" and regularly kept under surveillance by the civil and literary police concerned about its depravity, actually promulgated a message and an ethic founded to a great extent on those very values it appeared to bring under attack. Bourgeois life during the Third Republic had done a rather good job of hiding its seamier side beneath the dignity of bearded faces and the amplitude of feminine attire. Certain novelists such as Oscar Méténier, Dubut de La Forest, Jean Lorrain, and the young Rachilde devoted considerable talent and energy to peeling off these false beards and pulling up those skirts a bit further than was deemed permissible. The images of this lovely society that have come down to us through Nadar's legacy of charming photographs and Gustave Caillebotte's and Jean Beraud's meticulous canvases have been somewhat impugned—raped, some might say—by these iconoclastic novelists and a host of even lesser-known colleagues.

The rehabilitation of Jean Lorrain's work has gotten well underway over the past fifteen years or so, primarily because of the efforts of the late Philippe Jullian and those of Pierre Kyria, Christian Berg, and Michel Desbruères, among others. It now appears to be the turn of his contemporary and faithful friend, Rachilde. Since 1984, a number of major studies of this author have come from Claude Dauphine, Micheline Besnard-Coursodon, Robert Ziegler, and Melanie Hawthorne, all of them decisively underscoring a shift in critical approach characterized by rigorous and sustained objectivity.[1] From these nevertheless diverse evaluations a common premise emerges: that readers, especially males, should guard against jumping to the conclusion that the stratagems of Rachilde's protagonists are perverse. A person such as Raoule de Vénérande, heroine or hero, as one may choose to think, of the novel *Monsieur Vénus*, or another such as Mary

Barbe, the "Marquise de Sade" of the novel by the same name, are likely to seem perverse if the reader refuses to understand that their attitudes and actions reveal, in the final analysis, that Western society has almost always adopted a double standard in judging human conduct. The person who begins to think and act in a manner fitting the stereotype of the opposite sex may seem perverse for having dared tamper with prevailing standards. What is true for many of Rachilde's most "shocking" female characters also holds true for a man such as Paul-Eric de Fertzen, one of the major characters of her novel *Les Hors-nature*, whom Huysmans, in an unpublished letter to Rachilde, described as *"une sirène dextrement campée"*[2] ("a skillfully presented siren"). But the question is a much broader one; far from being limited to patterns of dress and physical mannerisms, the reversal of traditionally recognized male and female roles extends to intellectual attitudes and to reasoning, two realms in which much more serious reader disorientation is likely to occur.

Until very recently, literary critics have almost universally relegated Rachilde's work to the backwaters of modern French letters. In his history of French literature published just after World War II and seven years before Rachilde's death, Henri Clouard pigeonholed her in the *"coin des démoniaques"*[3] ("the demonics' corner"). As Melanie Hawthorne has rightly pointed out in her article on gender roles in *Monsieur Vénus*, the scorn that critics have heaped upon Rachilde even in very recent times is almost invariably based upon the erroneous perception that her novels are little more than gratuitous descriptions of monstrous sexual deviations. Maurice Barrès, writing, presumably in way of promotion, the preface to the first French edition of *Monsieur Vénus* in 1889, had the dubious honor of being the first to shunt critics off in this direction. Our perspective one hundred years later allows for a somewhat more objective appraisal of the alleged perversities which we see as the radical means adopted by Rachilde to condemn what she perceived as equally monstrous abuses of women's rights, the principles of patriotism, honor, marriage, and a host of other cornerstones of French and Western civilization. By enthralling—or disgusting—us with the excesses of her heroes and heroines, Rachilde deftly suggests, and without being in the least didactic, that these "monsters" of hers have been produced not so much by bourgeois principles as by the shameless perversion of these values by men and women who proclaim themselves to be the defenders of the nation, women's honor, the family, and so forth. The more outrageous the abuse seems to Rachilde the more she ups the ante by inventing characters and aberrations that for her time were definitely beyond the pale.

In her novels published between 1880 and 1900, Marguerite Eym-
ery, writing under the pseudonym Rachilde as well as the anagram of
this pseudonym, Jean *de Chilra*,[4] applied her talents to the parody, not
so much of bourgeois values as of their abuse at the hands of a vicious
and hypocritical society. With such slaps in society's face as *Monsieur
Vénus* (1884), *La Marquise de Sade* (1887), and *Les Hors-nature* (1897),
Rachilde espoused both feminist and homosexual causes, as well as the
cause of "honest" people, supposing there were any. Love, country,
conjugal fidelity, maternity, and paternity are targets of Rachilde's
satire only to the extent that these values have been flouted by hosts of
such preposterous puppets as those exemplified by the regiment under
the command of Mary Barbe's father on the eve of the Franco-
Prussian war; or by heads of families who parade their conjugal
infidelity before others; or by parents who are incapable of setting for
their children the example of a united and loving couple. The dearth
of real parents is underscored by the large number of orphans, semi-
orphans, and bastards in Rachilde's early novels. Raoule de Vénérande, the heroine of *Monsieur Vénus,* is without parents; and the
precociously cruel young woman labeled the "Marquise de Sade"
(Mary Barbe) is the legitimate fruit of a union so corrupted by
hypocrisy and irresponsibility that she grows up very much on her
own. Her painful childhood is little more than the uninterrupted
observation of the cruelty, pettiness, and duplicity of adults. Continually uprooted by the clocklike reassignments of her father's regiment, the child will come to know but a single important emotional
anchor, and that is her innocent but already sadistic love for a poor
working-class boy who is, of course, a real orphan. After this helter-
skelter upbringing, completely devoid of parental affection, Mary is at
length emancipated by the death of her parents and married at the age
of eighteen to a Parisian aristocrat, a fast-living baron who at forty
thinks he has had enough of the company of money-grubbing courtesans. On their wedding night, the young baroness loses no time
avenging herself of her father's lack of affection and innumerable
despicable actions; she informs her husband that she will never love
him, nor will she grant him the hope of a legitimate heir:

> Oh, I have some strange theories, but you must resign yourself to them,
> Sir. It so happens that I don't care to create others who will suffer some day
> as I've suffered. . . . As for this God-given maternity bestowed on every
> girl who surrenders to her husband, well, I exhaust its tremendous tender-
> ness at the sacred moment that leaves us still free *not* to procreate, free *not*
> to bestow death while bestowing life, free to exempt from filth and despair
> one who has done nothing to merit such fate. Let me put it to you

cynically: I don't choose to be a mother, first of all because I don't want to suffer, and next because I don't wish to cause suffering.[5]

Having taken such a position, she quickly adopts imperious attitudes towards everyone about her and gains authority over some, including an elderly uncle who had been her guardian before her marriage. This distinguished Parisian scientist and professor of medicine will opt for suicide as a result of the carefully dosed torture administered by his former charge who had applied herself first to seducing her uncle, then to rejecting him disdainfully.

In Mary Barbe's protest against a phallocratic society, a dual goal rapidly becomes apparent: first, to wreak vengeance on the male of the species; second, to cast off all bonds of servitude or any attitude perceived as such. According to the novelistic focus Rachilde proposes, the reader is expected to take Mary Barbe as the real victim, who in turn makes victims of her own in the name of all women. The author generally chooses as the butt of ridicule pompous, even stupid men wholly lacking the finesse of sentiment and tormented intelligence with which she so generously endows her heroines. The Marquise de Sade indeed triumphs, but over male creatures so naive and abject that her victory scarcely deserves that name. The tactics in this one-sided struggle are the very ones that had been employed by young Mary's cat Minoute, who scratched and drew her little mistress's blood. Robert Ziegler, in his study of this novel, has underscored the importance of the cat's claws which allow for "cutting, scratching, stabbing [that] can be done more surreptitiously" (117). The mores of this supposedly domesticated animal, preserving as they do a certain savagery, admirably sum up the case of Mary Barbe.

As for the imbrication of bourgeois values in all these diabolical arts, it would be difficult to cite a better example than the love affair of Raoule de Vénérande and Jacques Silvert in *Monsieur Vénus*. As Besnard-Coursodon has rightly observed: *"Non seulement la 'normalité' hétérosexuelle est effacée"* ("not only is heterosexual 'normality' wiped out")—since Raoule plays the man's role and Jacques the woman's—but homosexuality too is *"dépassée par la perversion, qui est complète . . . [et] qui rétablit l'apparence d'un couple 'normal' [minant] en fait la norme de la nature"* ("exceeded by perversion, which is complete . . . [and] which restores the appearance of a 'normal' couple, thus in fact [subverting] nature's norm") (123). It should be added, however, that the very fact that Rachilde is aiming here at an appearance of normality, even in parody, brings us back to a kind of bourgeois equilibrium, since the two roles *are* reversed. Heterosexuality of a sort is indeed preserved, but at what a price! The self-criticism implied in the very nature of parody, since it allows for reinterpretation of what it has itself proposed, would seem to apply here, as in other "outrageous" situations concocted by Rachilde. By attacking abuse with abuse she underscores one of the tenets of Decadence.[6]

Mary Barbe, at the opposite pole from Raoule de Vénérande and in a less dramatic way, joins forces with bourgeois values through her almost total lack of visible revolt against appearances and ritual. She does *not* flaunt her incestuous liaison with her husband's bastard son; she *does* go into mourning for her elderly uncle whom she has effectively pushed into suicide—she always takes into account what other people will say, just as any submissive woman of her day would do. This feline-woman relishes her cruel pleasures all the more that they remain secret ones. By pursuing a line of conduct that is the opposite of Raoule de Vénérande's, by dissimulating her true feelings and motives, this young Marquise de Sade actually seems, to those who know her only superficially, to be very much like the bourgeois and aristocratic women for whom she actually harbors nothing but scorn. In the true tradition of the bourgeois who desire nothing more than to distinguish themselves from other bourgeois, Mary Barbe gives this somewhat ironic turn of the screw by striving to make her mendacious conformity the *sine qua non* of her secret revolt. The transvestite note that creeps into several scenes of *La Marquise de Sade* is a much more obvious theme in *Monsieur Vénus* and *Les Hors-nature*. As is the case in many of Jean Lorrain's novels, transvestism, so far from being an exceptional element, is rather the expression of a tendency which in *fin-de-siècle* literature approached something like an artistic fashion. "*Fin de siècle, fin de sexe*" ("end of century, end of sex") Jean Lorrain cynically opined. His brash quip at least has the merit of suggesting quite succinctly the sacrifices to an aesthetic mode that d'Annunzio and Debussy, among others, were prepared to make in their *Martyre de Saint-Sébastien*, incarnated not by a man but by a bosomless, boyish Ida Rubenstein. Similar sacrifices at the same altar were frequently and willingly performed by Richard Strauss, whose predilection for mezzo-sopranos in men's garb is confirmed in some of his finest operas, such as *Der Rosenkavalier* (in which there is even travesty of disguise in the first and third acts), *Arabella*, and *Ariadne auf Naxos*.[7] In passing, let us not forget the example of Sarah Bernhardt as the Aiglon or as Pierrot.[8] Paintings of this period frequently follow a similar course in the frail personages of indeterminate sex who preside, often with hieratic gestures, over the melancholy or cataclysmic scenes conceived by Odilon Redon and Gustave Moreau. Joséphin Péladan also adds a pseudoscientific note with his dissertations on the androgyne. But in all his theoretical poses, Sâr Péladan seems more attuned to asexuality than to bisexuality. And that is precisely one of the messages that Jean Lorrain was attempting to convey with his stinging rejoinder: *"Fin de siècle, fin de sexe."* He doubtless also had in mind other more popular and more concrete manifestations of sexual indecision and confusion: for example, masked balls, carnival, and the ever more brazen exhibitionism of the Miss Sacripants that Proust would soon describe in studying aspects of Odette de Crécy and her kind, such as Lucie Delarue-Mardrus, Romaine Brooks, Colette, and the famous "amazone" Natalie Clifford Barney.[9]

The other side of the coin in matters of disguise shows the effigies of such characters as Adelsward de Fersen, the hero of a future novel by Roger Peyrefitte, *L'Exilé de Capri;* vaporous Pierre Lotis; and many another Baron de Charlus bent on putting the dogs on the wrong scent. As literary subjects, the coin was to prove to be worth its weight in gold in the closing years of the nineteenth century. And Rachilde, more resolutely and earlier than most, set about exploiting this vein of gold, or perhaps of quicksilver, more properly speaking. Indeed, well before Jung she seized on the importance of the symbolism of Mercurius, creating as she did a menagerie of intriguing monsters, all of whom possess that antinomian dual nature that Jung has analyzed as basic to Mercurius[10] and in which the masculine and the feminine elements undergo strange metamorphoses. In a Jungian archetypal reading of the three Rachilde novels previously mentioned, one is impressed by the manner in which she exploits the Mercurius symbol, whether consciously or otherwise. The fundamental dualism of the principal characters stands out first and foremost, followed by their interdependence and the role reversibility of each of the members of the three couples in question.

It will be recalled that in *Monsieur Vénus* the couple is composed of an imperious young woman with masculine bearing, Raoule de Vénérande, and the all-too-handsome Jacques Silvert, whom she seduces, subjugates and effectively turns into her "mistress." In *La Marquise de Sade*, Mary Barbe, after having married a baron whom she proceeds to tame on their wedding night, as we have seen, loses no time seducing his bastard son, a young medical student. She quickly reduces the latter to near total dependency, playing with him and his emotions like a cat with a mouse. For his willpower and ambition she substitutes and imposes incestuous pleasures that she seasons with sadistic and vampiric condiments. His whole existence is soon circumscribed by the sphere of satisfaction of their sexual appetites. *Femme fatale* if ever there was one, Mary Barbe uses her fingernails like a cat's claws to exact their toll in the couple's caresses. In her secret, nocturnal visits to the apartment where she keeps her male victim—reversing once again the more prevalent arrangement—her thirst for his blood truly designates her as the incarnation of the "Sirène repue" ("Satiated Siren") depicted by the turn-of-the-century artist Gustav Adolphe Mossa.[11]

Finally in *Les Hors-nature* the couple in question is composed of the two brothers, Reutler and Paul-Eric de Fertzen. Like his father a Prussian, Reutler has been striving all his life to repress his homosexual tendencies through total abstinence. He is tall, well-built, and of a very sober demeanor. On the other hand, his younger brother, Paul-Eric, who was born in France during the 1870 war, has inherited the fragile beauty of their French mother, who died in childbirth. Realizing quite early that Paul-Eric's temperament is much too feminine, the elder brother devotes his life and their considerable fortune to educating Paul-Eric in what he takes to be the "proper" manner, that is to say he throws the adolescent boy into the arms of Parisian courtesans and Egerias with the expectation of remedying his lack of virile attributes. But through the bewilderingly improbable developments of this drama, the younger brother's true nature remains unshaken and in the end wins out over such paltry remedies. He becomes more effeminate with each passing day. Reutler, himself the victim of his double betrayal of nature, is forced to recognize that his own punishment is to have fallen hopelessly in love with his brother. Much like Raoule de Vénérande and Mary Barbe, Reutler has up to this point always associated the concept of true love with abstinence. This man—whose firmness of purpose and manner and whose self-denial holds others at bay—could well subscribe tacitly to the motto carved over Mary Barbe's bed: *"Aimer, c'est souffrir"* ("To love is to suffer"). But Reutler goes further still, and, in the final expression of his overpowering and desperate love for his brother, effectively transforms the motto into: *"Aimer, c'est mourir"* ("To love is to die"). Everything exacerbates the awkward situation which for too long a time has prevailed between the brothers in their strange and estranged existence in the lonely family castle; to go on living in this way under the same roof is out of the question, as is a return to Paris and its follies. For this improbable and chaste couple with their dreams of the impossible only one solution remains, and that is to disappear in an apotheosis worthy of *Die Götterdämmerung*, the conflagration of their isolated Walhalla. In a letter to Rachilde, Huysmans dubs this denouement *"sardanapalesque"*; then, in a rather long and flattering enumeration of the qualities he discovers in this novel, he warmly congratulates the author on having created such a character as Reutler: *"Car celui-là vous l'avez animé d'une sorte de souffle mystérieux et d'une grandeur épique . . . il reste inoubliable, avec son air souffrant, son rictus, ses yeux d'eau noire, toute l'énigme de son orgueil. Il emporte tout dans son sillage car il apparaît comme inconnu avant vous, comme jamais vu"*[12] ("for you have endowed this character with a kind of mysterious breath and an epic grandeur . . . he is unforgettable with his suffering attitude, his gaping grin, his liquid black eyes, and the whole enigma of his pride. He sweeps aside everything in his path; he appears like something that was unknown before you, like something never seen before"). A most flattering comment, to be sure, but not quite exact. A similar love that "sweeps aside everything in its path" can be found in a previous novel by Rachilde, entitled, as it happens, *A Mort (1886)*. The heroine, Berthe Soirès, attempts as Reutler does, to reinvent love, is overwhelmed by her superhuman effort, wastes away and dies in a kind of *Liebestod*.

In choosing to give the protagonists of *Les Hors-nature* the names Reutler and Paul-Eric de Fertzen, Rachilde seems to allude somewhat obliquely to the many rebuffs and disappointments suffered by her contemporary, count Adelsward de Fersen, a most celebrated example of the "bric-à-brac gréco-préraphaélitico modern' style"—Cocteau *dixit*—that provided cocktail conversation topics and tabloid "scoops" around the turn of the century. Jean Lorrain, too, had a nose for such game and was obviously fascinated by it, as evidenced in several of his journalistic pieces and short stories that beat around the subject of Adelsward de Fersen's life style without, however, quite daring to tackle the matter of homosexuality directly. The same timidity did not keep him from treating the subject of lesbianism, as evidenced in his novel *Maison pour dames*, a story whose intrigue hinges on the competition for a literary prize to be awarded to a woman poet and on the recruitment procedures used to attract applicants. Again because of a dual standard working in reverse, as it were, and for once to the woman's advantage, can we really be surprised that the intrepid Rachilde, the same young woman that Lorrain addresses in a letter as *"Chère Hermaphrodite"*[13] (Dear Hermaphrodite") approaches the subject of homosexuality with relative ease in *Les Hors-nature?* From the beginning of her appearance on the literary scene she had resolutely decided to throw off her provincial origin and to hitch her wagon to the Parisian star. Claude Dauphine has expressed it most forcefully: *"Cette intrusion de 'La Fille aux yeux d'or' chez 'Eugénie Grandet' est révélatrice de l'optique de Rachilde: plutôt Sodome et Gomorrhe qu'une sous-prefecture. Hors de Paris, point de vie!"* ("This intrusion of 'The Girl with the Golden Eyes' into Eugenie Grandet's domain is revealing of Rachilde optics: Better to be in Sodom and Gomorrah than in some provincial backwater. Outside of Paris, nothing doing!") (p. 18).

Equivocal dualism, interdependence, reversibility of gender roles: these are the three characteristics associated in these three novels of

Rachilde with sensual and physical love, as is the spirit Mercurius in his metaphysical and incorporeal sense. Jung tells us that "for the alchemists, as we know not only from the ancient but also from the later writers, Mercurius as the arcane substance had a more or less secret connection with the goddess of love" and that in certain representations "Aphrodite appears with a vessel from the mouth of which pours a ceaseless stream of quicksilver" (p. 216–17). Other aspects of this spirit emphasized by Jung and that are striking in Rachilde's protagonists are a "many-sided, changeable, and deceitful" nature and the fact that this spirit "enjoys equally the company of the good and the wicked" (p. 217).

As a woman writer, then, Rachilde could doubtless afford to treat a subject such as *Les Hors-nature,* if not with impunity then at least without too much fear of reprisal from a certain literate public, the very one that showed far less tolerance of Jean Lorrain's sallies onto the same terrain. And Rachilde's relatively more favorable treatment was due not solely to the fact that she was a woman, but was in even larger part due to the narrative voice she adopts, permitting preservation of a certain distance and objectivity, two advantages that Jean Lorrain's much more personal style is surely lacking, his *La Maison Philibert* being a prime example. The exceptional adventures of the two de Fertzen brothers in *Les Hors-nature* may astound or intrigue us; they can not move us, let alone give the illusion of real events, as do Lorrain's novels. It is precisely this detachment and this hypothetical bent that allowed Rachilde to tackle broad matters of human behavior in general, and of sexuality in particular, without bringing down storms of critical invective as Lorrain did. Among her many merits as a novelist, more recognition is due her for having dared to put her finger squarely on an area of widespread medical error in the late nineteenth century, one that caused endless problems for such individuals as the young André Gide and for Marcel Proust throughout his life: *"La névrose, la monomanie? Cela n'existe qu'en faisant dévier une creature de sa ligne."* ("Neurosis and monomania? They come about only by causing a creature to deviate from its bent"), she wrote in *Les Hors-nature.*[14] It is understood here that the bent is homosexuality; in Reutler de Fertzen's case without a trace of effeminate mannerism, in that of his brother, exaggerated effeminacy. Reutler finally grasps, but much too late, the fact that from the outset he should have accepted his own nature as well as his brother's, without attempting to "correct" them. *"N'est-il pas bien plus contre la nature,"* he says, *"de résister désespérément à ses instincts?"* ("Is it not much more unnatural to resist desperately one's instincts?") (p. 58–59). An affirmative answer to his question is given in dramatic fashion through the disastrous events recorded in the final pages of this novel.

Notes

1. Claude Dauphiné, *Rachilde, femme de lettres 1900* (Périgueux: Pierre Fanlac, 1985); Micheline Besnard-Coursodon, "*Monsieur Vénus, Madame Adonis:* sexe et discours," *Littérature*, 54 (1984), 121–27; Robert Ziegler, "Rachilde and 'l'amour compliqué'," *Atlantis*, 11:2 (1986), 115–24; Melanie Hawthorne, "*Monsieur Vénus:* A Critique of Gender Roles," *NCFS*, 16:1–2 (1987–88), 162–79. Further reference to these works will be given in parentheses.

2. Manuscript letter from Huysmans to Rachilde dated 14 March 1897, belonging to the Humanities Research Center, University of Texas at Austin.

3. Henri Clouard, *Histoire de la littérature française depuis le symbolisme jusqu'à nos jours*, 2 vols. (Paris: Albin Michel, 1947–49) 1:173.

4. Her novel *L'Heure sexuelle* (1898) was so signed. See Will L. McLendon, "*Autour d'une lettre inédite de Rachilde à Huysmans*," *Bulletin de la Société J.-K. Huysmans*, 20. 75 (1983), 21–24.

5. *Oh! j'ai des théories bizarres, mais il faut vous resigner, Monsieur. Il ne me plaît pas, moi, de faire des êtres qui souffriront un jour ce que j'ai souffert . . . La maternité que le Créateur enseigne à chaque fille qui se livre à l'époux, moi, j'épuise son immensité de tendresse à cette minute sacrée qui nous laisse encore libre de ne pas procréer, libre de ne pas donner la mort en donnant la vie, libre d'exclure de la fange et du désespoir celui qui n'a rien fait pour y tomber. Je vous dis cyniquement: je ne veux pas être mère, d'abord parce que je ne veux pas souffrir, ensuite parce que je ne veux pas faire souffrir.*" Rachilde, *La Marquise de Sade* (Paris: E. Monnier, 1887), 278. Further reference will be given in parentheses.

6. For a detailed consideration of this principle see Michele Hannoosh, *Parody and Decadence* (Columbus: Ohio State University Press, 1989).

7. Opera-goers today are being acquainted with another "assault" on their values, an oral rather than a visual one, in the return of counter-tenors who, in the absence of modern *castrati*, are insuring a certain authenticity in the interpretation of Handel's operas (*Giulio Cesare*, for example). Resistance to these efforts and to Philip Glass's use of the counter-tenor in his opera *Akhnaten* would seem to indicate that the public more easily accepts one directional travesty, i.e., women in male roles. Hearing a high soprano voice emanate from a man's mouth is apparently more disconcerting.

8. Giuseppe de Nittis's portrait of Sarah Bernhardt as Pierrot now hangs in the Elizabeth McNey Museum in San Antonio.

9. See her biography by Jean Chalon, *Portrait d'une séductrice* (Paris: Stock, 1976).

10. C. G. Jung, *Alchemical Studies*, in *The Collected Works of C. G. Jung*, Bollingen Series, 20 vols. (Princeton, N.J.: Princeton University Press, 1967) 13: 216. Further reference to this volume will be given in parentheses.

11. This work is in the Jules Chéret Museum in Nice.

12. Manuscript letter of 14 March 1897, in The Humanities Research Center, University of Texas at Austin with whose kind authorization we quote.

13. A letter catalogued by Jean Le Bodo, director of *Biblis* (Paris: Librairie du Vieux Colombier, n.d.) 533. We are not aware if this letter has been published.

14. (Paris: Mercure de France, 1897), 308. Further reference to this novel will be given in parentheses.

PART 2
Voices and/in Dialogue

Prophetic Utterance and Irony in *Trois contes*

KAREN L. ERICKSON

Prophecy is a recurrent voice in Flaubert's collection of tales, and provides a parabolic narrative model for a kind of textual transmission rooted in historical social commentary—the visionary challenge to a community through the voice of a prophet.[1] In this paper, I will examine the role of the prophet in *Trois contes*, the ways in which prophetic utterances affect narrative structure, and the role of irony in the process of challenging the characters continually to reinterpret the meaning of prophecy and of their very nature. I use the term "irony" here to mean the progressive revelation to a character of a misunderstanding or limitation, often involving a recognition of hubris. Looking at irony this way, we see parallels between prophecy and irony. Prophetic discourse points ahead to a textual "future," and implies an external authority, the source of the prophecy. Irony also invokes a more complete knowledge, a different narrative perspective, in its disclosure of the dissonance between reality and appearance. The use of these devices complicates issues of narrative coherence and voice, and reveals in the text elements of social criticism.

Prophecy in *Trois contes* presents a variable presence, but in all three tales there are voices of revelation which share certain characteristics, evoke similar reactions in those hearing the voices, and set in motion a progression from misinterpretation to correction to new interpretation. The prophetic voice is most apparent in the third tale, "*Hérodias*," which recounts the events surrounding the death of the biblical figure of John the Baptist, Iaokanann. His diatribes follow the model and evoke the wrath of the ancient Hebrew prophets. He is imprisoned in the depths of Hérode's citadel; nonetheless his voice travels freely and mystically. It reveals the crimes of incest, murder, and assassination, and predicts continued sterility and impending deaths. The fact that nothing can stop this unusual voice distinguishes it from the efforts of Phanuel and Hérodias, who show considerable powers of divination in their attempts to read the inevitable in signs and stars. Phanuel's messages, one of which is that an important man will die that night, are continually interrupted, which adds to the suspense of the story. The tale develops suspense, as well, in the theme of departure and return, through its portrayal of debates about the resurrection, the return of the prophet Elijah, the coming of the Son of David. Prophecy is central to the main intrigues: the possible renunciation of Hérodias and Salomé's consequent training and dance, the political attacks on Hérode's power, the death of Iaokanann.

In *"Hérodias,"* prophecy is not a private, potentially imaginary or hallucinatory incident but a social interaction. The prophet's message is repeated, translated, free to spread beyond its context, beyond the citadel, beyond its own narrative. This enrages Hérodias, terrifies Hérode, frustrates Mannaëi, entrances the Romans, seduces Phanuel, revives the people's image of their exile; it functions in different ways in the characters' various private dramas. The classical containment of time and place in this story contributes to the pressure on the various events, desires and subplots. The overabundance of narrative possibilities and potential outcomes is illustrated in the reactions to Iaokanann's voice. The narrative suggests, through Hérode's search for a scapegoat, that one single death could satisfy everyone and fulfill the various elliptical statements repeated throughout the story. The characters expect certain results from the prophecy, and from the death of this man, but such expectations bring narrative silence, not freedom, for those who sought to cut off prophetic language at its source, or at what they thought was its source. The many factions and enemies present at the banquet are represented as members of an antique world which is passing. At the end of the tale, the characters are divided into those who believe and those who do not. The latter are left within the citadel, the isolated and solitary place of the story. For the believers, there is an escape or departure, as the disciples leave carrying Iaokanann's head with them. In representing this remnant, Flaubert shows in an understated manner the profound compulsion to save something from the death of time's passing and the resolution of endings, though no key is offered for how one escapes decline, or fate, or death.

In the second tale, *"La Légende de saint Julien l'Hospitalier,"* the prophetic voice has a more legendary, mystical character. Three voices offer prophecies: A hermit speaks to Julien's mother during the night and has the unearthly character of a supernatural speaker, both in his words and in his presence and disappearance—he predicts her son will be a saint. A gypsy outside the castle speaks to the father, predicting worldly glory. The mother says nothing of the prediction of sainthood for fear of being seen as proud; the father says nothing of the prediction of worldly power for fear of being ridiculed. Yet they both await the outcome of their separate predictions. The words of the black stag, who addresses Julien in the forest, become the foundation for the central scene of the tale (central in structure as well as plot). His pronouncement, *"Maudit! Maudit! Maudit! Un jour, coeur féroce, tu assassineras ton père et ta mère!"*[2] ("Accursed! Accursed! Accursed! One day, cruel heart, you will kill your father and mother!") introduces the specific threat of parricide, as well as the underlying preoccupation with damnation and salvation. This is the legend of a *saint*; Julien must absolutely reach sainthood. The title, like the prophetic messages, informs the progress of the story, as it introduces expectations of a certain kind of fulfillment.

In contrast to the social character and repeated quotation of Iaokanann's prophetic utterances in *"Hérodias,"* the predictions in *"La Légende"* remain (with one significant exception) within the individual experience of the different characters, who keep hidden from each other their potentially mystical encounter with prophetic speakers. The lack of communication in this realm contributes both to the suspense of the intrigue and to the actual working-out of the narrative. When Julien finally confides in his wife, telling her of the stag's words and of his fear of fulfilling them, a prophetic utterance is passed on to a third party for the first time. Her reaction is to reason with him, to analyze the utterance within a logical context:

> [. . .] *enfin, un jour, il avoua son horrible pensée.*
>
> *Elle la combattait, en raisonnant très bien: son père et sa mère, probablement, étaient morts; si jamais il les revoyait, par quel hasard, dans quel but, arriverait-il à cette abomination? Donc, sa crainte n'avait pas de cause, et il devait se remettre à chasser.*[3]

> ("But at last one day he told her of his dreadful fear. She fought against it, reasoning very soundly: his father and mother were probably dead; but if he were ever to see them again, what chance or purpose could possibly lead him to commit such a horrible crime? His fear was completely groundless, and he ought to take up hunting again.")

When Julien's parents arrive in an unlikely and (to the wife's logical reasoning) unpredictable meeting of principals, he is in fact out on a solitary hunt. In his absence, his wife becomes the intermediary in establishing identity and in interpreting the appropriate response to the prophetic utterance. She renders possible the realization of the prophecy in part by placing them in her own bed, as a mark of honor, in part by not communicating in turn her knowledge of Julien's fear: *"Ils firent mille questions sur Julien. Elle répondait à chacune, mais eut soin de taire l'idée funèbre qui les concernait."*[4] ("They asked her countless questions about Julien. She answered every one, but was careful

not to mention the gloomy obsession in which they were concerned.")
Julien arrives in the darkness before dawn to feel two bodies asleep in
his bed. He thinks his wife is with another man, kills his parents in a
murderous rage, thus fulfilling the prophecy.

When Julien's wife appears at the door with a lighted candle, *"elle
comprit tout"* ("she took everything in"), and in horror drops the
candle which Julien picks up. By its light he recognizes his parents.
His wife contributes both to the fulfillment of the crime and to his
realization of its nature, participating in the progressive and therefore
partial revelation of the prophetic utterance. Though this scene seems
to fulfill the prophecy, the tale continues as Julien recounts his story
and seeks salvation. This comes finally in the form of a mystical
leper—with an uncanny voice, glowing eyes, compelling demands—
who asks the sacrifice of Julien's life. He provides an answer, not to the
prediction of assassination, but to the threat of damnation. Julien
becomes a saint.

At first reading, *"Un Coeur simple"* presents no prophet figure.
However, in comparison with these other voices, we see that the kinds
of speech, linguistic problems, and misinterpretations presented in
Trois contes are introduced and find a first voice in Loulou, the parrot.
The prophetic speakers in the last two tales are characterized by voices
with unusual volume, character and attraction, blazing eyes, a solemn
stance. In *"La Légende,"* the hermit speaks *"sans desserer les lèvres"*
("without opening his lips"), the gypsy has *"les prunelles flamboyantes"*
("blazing eyes"), the stag also speaks *"les yeux flamboyants, solennel
comme un patriarche et comme un justicier"* ("with blazing eyes, solemn
as a patriarch or a judge"). The Leper's voice reaches Julien across a
great distance and through a storm; he is described thus: *"la figure
pareille à un masque de plâtre et les deux yeux plus rouges que des
charbons"* ("his face like a plaster mask and his two eyes redder than
burning coals"); at the end of the legend, the Leper's eyes *"tout à coup
prirent une clarté d'étoiles"* ("all at once his eyes took on the brightness
of the stars"). In *"Hérodias,"* Iaokanann also is portrayed with blazing
eyes and roaring voice: *"Ses prunelles flamboyaient; sa voix rugissait"*
("His eyes flashed, his voice roared"), and his voice defies containment. For example, his long diatribe begins with a sigh audible
throughout the citadel: *"Ce fut d'abord un grand soupir, poussé d'une
voix caverneuse. Hérodias l'entendit à l'autre bout du palais. Vaincue par
une fascination, elle traversa la foule; et elle écoutait"* ("First, in a
sepulchral voice, there came a great sigh. Herodias heard it at the
other end of the palace. Yielding to an irresistible urge, she made her
way through the crowd and bent forward to listen"). As the diatribe
continues, Iaokanann's face *"avait l'air d'une broussaille, où étincelaient
deux charbons"* ("looked like a mass of brushwood in which two live

coals were glowing"). Finally, the voice completely escapes realistic bounds: *"La voix grossissait, se développait, roulait avec des déchirements de tonnerre, et, l'écho dans la montagne la répétant, elle foudroyait Machaerous d'éclats multipliés"* ("The voice grew louder and stronger, rolling and roaring like thunder, and as the mountains sent it back, it broke over Machaerus in repeated echoes").

In comparing Flaubert's portrayal of Loulou, we see that the parrot shares the uncanny volume and attraction of his voice and a peculiar light in his eye, as if Loulou were a lesser version of a prophetic speaker: *"Les éclats de sa voix bondissaient dans la cour, l'écho les répétait"* ("his shrieks rang round the courtyard, the echo repeated them"). After Loulou's death and return as a stuffed parrot, his glass eye interacts with the light and with Félicité's devotion: *"Quelquefois, le soleil entrant par la lucarne frappait son oeil de verre, et en faisait jaillir un grand rayon lumineux qui la mettait en extase"* ("Sometimes the sun, as it came through the little window, caught his glass eye, so that it shot out a great luminous ray which sent her into ecstasies").[5] Though it is a caricature, the parrot comes to represent the voice of God which speaks in the descent of the Spirit in Félicité's deformed theology. She can hear this voice long after she is deaf to human speech, and attends to his utterances with reverence. The parrot, capable of repeating meaningful sounds, is almost by definition a figure for unusual or random revelation, ironic disclosure, comical misinterpretation, and speaks as if in parody of the prophetic voices which follow in the collection. This simple voice, however, is profoundly appropriate for the nature of crime and belief set forth in the first tale.

Loulou's prophetic utterance is linked to the irony that reveals the reality, the human limitations beneath appearances. In the tradition of Merlin's laughter (the laughter of the prophet who sees through pretense to recognize secret plots and future events, and who signals his prophetic insight through laughter[6]), the parrot laughs at Bourais (Mme. Aubain's financial advisor) long before any question of his propriety is raised in the story:

La figure de Bourais, sans doute, lui paraissait très drôle. Dès qu'il l'apercevait, il commençait à rire, à rire de toutes ses forces. Les éclats de sa voix bondissaient dans la cour, l'écho les répétait, les voisins se mettaient à leurs fenêtres, riaient aussi; et, pour n'être pas vu du perroquet, M. Bourais se coulait le long du mur, en dissimulant son profil avec son chapeau, atteignait la rivière, puis entrait par la porte du jardin; et les regards qu'il envoyait à l'oiseau manquaient de tendresse.[7]

("Bourais's face obviously struck him as terribly funny, for as soon as he saw it he was seized with uncontrollable laughter. His shrieks rang round the courtyard, the echo repeated them, and the neighbors came to their windows and started laughing, too. To avoid being seen by the bird, M. Bourais used to creep along the wall, hiding his face behind his hat, until he got to the river, and then come into the house from the garden. The looks he gave the parrot were far from tender.")

The narrator does not give an authoritative interpretation of the seemingly inexplicable laughter; the explanation, "Bourais's face obviously struck him as very funny" is limited by *"sans doute"*— "probably, obviously." Like Julien's wife, the narrator reasons with this odd voice and seeks a reasonable explanation. Something in this scene is peculiar, and unresolved. Bourais hides from Loulou, slinking around *"en dissimulant son profil avec son chapeau"* ("hiding his face behind his hat") just as Hérodias hides her face when Iaokanann sees her:

Dés qu'il m'aperçut, il cracha sur moi toutes les malédictions des prophètes. Ses prunelles flamboyaient; sa voix rugissaient; il levait les bras, comme pour arracher le tonnerre. Impossible de fuir! [. . .] je m'éloignais lentement, m'abritant sous mon manteau, glacée par ces injures qui tombaient comme une pluie d'orage.[8]

("As soon as he saw me, he spat all the curses of the prophets at me. His eyes flashed, his voice roared, and he raised his arms as if to pluck thunder out of the sky. It was impossible to get away from him. [. . .] I moved off slowly, cowering under my cloak, my blood running cold at the insults that were raining down on me.")

The repetition of vocabulary (*"Dès qu'il l'apercevait / Dès qu'il m'aperçut"*) and descriptive detail reinforces the correspondence between the two scenes. Characters are drawn to listen to the voice in spite of themselves; like the people in the citadel, the neighbors come to laugh along with Loulou, without understanding why they are laughing. When Bourais commits suicide upon the discovery of his fraud and wrongdoing, the narrative explains implicitly the reason for Loulou's laughter. This is also the work of a kind of irony, a peripeteia, reversal of fortune, that reveals the pettiness of the self-important human dimension. Through its laughter and through its decay, the bird signals the future material downfall of the household, as the stag and Iaokanann each predict the end of a family line. Though the narrative resolution of Loulou's prophetic utterance appears quite simple (the parrot laughs at Bourais; Bourais is unmasked as an unsavory character in contradiction with his image and standing in the bourgeois household and community), Loulou also plays a more and more central role in Félicité's problematic spiritual development, not unlike the Leper and Iaokanann in the other tales. The description of the parrot, his ambiguous relation to divinity, and his role in unveiling a hidden element or coarseness beneath the appearance of gentility and grace, the weakness hidden by a position of power, announce the more elaborate prophetic voices in the other tales.

When a narrative contains a prophecy of some future occurrence, there is an implicit narratological leap, an anticipation by the listener of the fulfillment of the prophecy. The suspense of waiting for the other piece of the puzzle, the scene of completion, can and often does dominate the narrative. In stories containing prophecies, from "Sleeping Beauty" to the Oedipus myth, the characters try to bring about or hinder the realization—to deflect, soften, or avoid altogether the prophesied outcome. Other narratives move without clearly recognizable prophecy, and only at the second scene are we aware that an anterior scene was indeed prophetic. It is this way that Loulou's laughter becomes prophetic, for only when Bourais is disgraced do we understand why the parrot laughed. Julien's wife understands, after the parricide, why her reasoning was powerless. Her understanding of her own participation in the event is ironic. In the final scene of *"Hérodias,"* Phanuel can interpret an obscure statement that Iaokanann made (*"Pour qu'il croisse, il faut que je diminue"* ["If he is to wax, then I must wane"]) only in the wake of the prophet's death, and with the unspecified news brought in from the outside. But even then, the tales refrain from any final judgment.

The multiplicity of possible interpretations indicates the ambiguity inherent in this type of expectation. Thinking that one interpretation resolves the prophecy, that one outcome verifies and dispenses with the prophecy, is the fundamental error[9]; Loulou's laughter refers to Bourais, but also to the stupidity of those who trust him. The work of repetition, quotation, interpretation of both the prophecy and its apparent fulfillment suggests that prophetic discourse is not an equation between pronouncement and realization but a continual reevaluation of potential. The citadel in *"Hérodias"* becomes a figure for the story itself, a place preparing to respond, but not yet ready to answer the riddle of its meaning. In the story of the Gordian knot, Alexander chose to cut the knot with his sword to answer the riddle. This may have led to domination, but the riddle contained in the knot was lost in the process. Prophecy in fiction offers this kind of mystery or riddle.

Prophecy and irony both depend upon perspective. Like the chorus in Greek tragedy, or an omniscient narrator, or the voice of irony, prophetic speech points to and challenges the limitations of narrative. In a sacred text, the authority of a divine source of prophecy (implied by the context of belief) calls for and guides interpretation. The authority of a prophetic voice in fiction lies partly within the narrator's scope, but partly beyond. The invocation by the prophet of an authority which knows a larger context and communicates in this parabolic fashion is a vehicle then for a kind of criticism, the revelation of truth; Flaubert's ironic portrayals of *"bêtise,"* the comparatively lucid powers of the prophetic voices, the urgency of harkening to this voice and the consequences of remaining deaf to it follow the tradition of Western prophetism. The prophetic perspective is linked ultimately with the external voice of commentary, with interpretation, and in many cases, with lament. Both prophecy and irony make explicit in the separation between utterance and revelation the desire for resolution and coherence, and challenge the characters', or the reader's, interpretation of a given event or statement. In the multiplicity of potential itineraries that prophecy ushers in, and in the progressive rejection of possible interpretations, these tales illustrate the ambiguity of meaning, the lack of control, the inevitable downfall of the proud. Flaubert's use of prophecy in *Trois contes* is evidence of a profound exploration of the potential of language.

Notes

1. Gustave Flaubert, *Trois contes*, ed. Edouard Maynial (Paris: Garnier Frères, 1969). All quotations from *Trois contes* will refer to this edition. All English translations are from Robert Baldick's translation (*Three Tales*, Baltimore, Maryland: Penguin, 1961).
Numerous critics have studied the religious aspects of the tales, most often through general concepts like sainthood or the Trinity. Two articles have a particular relevance to the question of prophecy: Carla Peterson, "The Trinity in Flaubert's *Trois contes:* Deconstructing History" (*French Forum*, 8 [1983], 243–58) and Ian Reid, "The Death of the Implied Author? Voice, Sequence and Control in Flaubert's *Trois contes"* (*Australian Journal of French Studies*, 23 [1986], 195–211). Raymonde Debray-Genette explores certain aspects of the subject in "Profane, Sacred: Disorder of Utterance in *Trois contes"* (in *Flaubert and Postmodernism*, ed. Naomi Schor et al. [Lincoln: University of Nebraska Press, 1984], 13–29). Susan Selvin's study, "Spatial Form in Flaubert's *Trois contes"* (*Romanic Review*, 74 [1983], 202–20) contains pertinent remarks that can be directly transposed from their slightly different context; the notion of epiphany is outlined by Emily Zants in "*Trois contes:* a New Dimension in Flaubert" (*Nottingham French Studies*, 18 [1979], 37–44). I discuss the characteristics of prophecy in secular texts in my doctoral dissertation, "Prophecy and Fulfillment in Flaubert's *Trois contes"* (Yale University, 1987). A fundamental study of the notion of prophecy as it is used here is Erich Auerbach's essay "Figura," in *Scenes from the Drama of European Literature* (Gloucester, Mass.: Peter Smith, 1973), especially 29–60.
2. *Trois contes*, 98.
3. Ibid., 108–9.
4. Ibid., 111. This type of narrative suspension is similar to the interrupted or

marginalized speech of Phanuel and Hérodias, and characterized by its limitation. Throughout *Trois contes* the tension between speech and silence becomes implicated in the tension between power and impotence.

5. Ibid., 66.

6. Paul Zumthor writes of this laughter: *"Le trait est digne de remarque, car c'est dans le folklore universel un thème très répandu: le sorcier éclate de rire au milieu des opérations magiques [. . .]. [Merlin] rit de la désillusion de ses compagnons et de la vanité de leurs efforts; dans la Vita, c'est qu'il a, seul des assistants, la prescience d'un ridicule caché, d'une situation paradoxale qui va se découvrir."* ("The trait is worthy of note, for it is a widely spread theme in universal folklore: The sorcerer bursts out laughing in the middle of magic operations [. . .]. [Merlin] laughs at the disillusionment of his companions and at the vanity of their efforts; in the *Vita*, he is the only one who has the foreknowledge of a hidden folly, or a paradoxical situation which is going to be revealed.") *Merlin le prophète* (Geneva: Slatkine Reprints, 1973), 45–46.

7. *Trois contes*, 53.

8. Ibid., 150–51.

9. Cf. Flaubert's remark in a letter to his friend Louis Bouilhet: *"L'ineptie consiste à vouloir conclure"* ("Stupidity consists in wanting to reach a conclusion"); as presented in *Préface à la vie d'écrivain: Extraits de la correspondance*, ed. Geneviève Bollème (Paris: Seuil, 1963), 52.

Baudelaire, Gautier, and *"une toilette savamment composée"*

SIMA GODFREY

On Sunday, 1 September 1867, a careful reader of *Le Figaro* might have come across the following news brief tucked away under the heading *"Hier—Aujourd'hui—Demain"* ("Yesterday—Today—Tomorrow"):

> *Charles Baudelaire agonisait hier soir, il est peut-être mort à l'heure qu'il est, en tout cas on craint qu'il ne passe pas la journée.*

> (Charles Baudelaire was in the last throes of death yesterday evening; at the present time he may well be dead; in any case, it is feared that he will not last the day.)

By the time the newspaper had come out, Charles Baudelaire, the poet, critic and occasional contributor to *Le Figaro*, was, in fact, dead. That same day, Charles Asselineau wrote to Auguste Poulet-Malassis, the poet's publisher and friend:

> *Mon cher ami,*
> *C'est fini. B. est mort hier à onze heures du matin après une longue agonie, mais douce et sans souffrance. Il était d'ailleurs si faible, qu'il ne luttait plus.*
> *Le service est pour [lundi]. J'ai tâché que nous ayons le plus de monde possible.[1]*

> (My dear friend,
> It is over. B. died yesterday at eleven A.M. after a long death-struggle, that was gentle still and without pain. He was, in fact, so weak that he had given up the fight.
> The service is set for [Monday]. I have tried to assemble as many people as possible.)

The reader of *Le Figaro* would have had to be very attentive indeed to spot the report on Baudelaire's deteriorating health; for in addition to being only one sentence long, it was sandwiched between two longer items of keen interest. The first, ironically enough, was a report on the overcrowded conditions in Paris cemeteries:

> *"Les cimetières de Paris sont pleins, la terre, saturée d'humus, ne peut plus absorber de cadavres, et il vient tous les jours des nouveaux. Où les mettre? M. le baron Haussmann nous le dira sans doute, mais le temps presse et il faut se presser."*

(The cemeteries of Paris are full; the ground, saturated with humus, can no longer absorb any more cadavers, and there are new ones coming in daily. Where to put them? Baron Haussmann will no doubt tell us, but time is short and we must find a speedy solution.)

This information boded ill for the poet who was dying in the next news item. Nevertheless, there is something apt about the morbid juxtaposition. The poet who had so identified his life with the crowding of Paris, was thus laid to rest, journalistically, right next to the crowded cemeteries that had haunted his mind:

> . . . *mon triste cerveau.*
> *C'est une pyramide, un immense caveau,*
> *Qui contient plus de morts que la fosse commune.*
> —*Je suis un cimetiére abhorré de la lune. . . .*

> . . . my brain.
> These branching catacombs, this pyramid
> contains more corpses than the potter's field:
> I am a graveyard that the moon abhors . . .)
>   ("Spleen, II" *Fleurs du Mal*, 76; trans. R. Howard)

Far more stunning for its ironies, however, was the lively entry that followed the news of the poet's agony. It was presented as a news flash from Baden-Baden:

> *Nous recevons de Bade la dépêche suivante:*
> *Bade, 31 août, 9h. 25m., Figaro, 3 rue Coq-Héron.*
> *Cora, hier soir, entrée Salons de la* Conversation, *dans une toilette tellement fantastique, tant de faux cheveux, tant de diamants, qu'elle a provoqué un fou rire.*
> *Bientôt foule compacte s'amasse autour.*
> *Petite émeute.*
> *Cora se retire . . . au bras de M. F . . . .*

(We have received from Baden-Baden the following dispatch:
Baden-Baden, 31 August, 9:25, *Figaro*, 3 rue Coq-Héron.
Cora, last night, made her entrance at the Salons of the
Conversation House, in such a fantastic toilette, so many
postiches in her hair, so many diamonds, that she provoked wild laughter.
Compact crowd soon gathered about.
Small riot.
Cora retires . . . on the arm of Mr. F . . . .)

The Cora in question was, of course, Cora Pearl, the notorious English-born courtesan of the Second Empire, and she clearly needed no introduction to readers of *Le Figaro*. She was at least as well-known for her wildly expensive and lavish toilettes as for her raucous manner and in fact stirred "quiet riots" everywhere she went. Whereas Charles Asselineau could only hope, in vain, to summon a respectable gathering at the funeral of Baudelaire, a single outfit worn by the infamous Cora was sure to draw a crowd. As he lay dying in a column of *Le Figaro*, Baudelaire, the poet, was thus eclipsed in print by a dazzling *toilette*.

Caught between the crowded cemeteries of Paris and a crowded fashion event in Baden-Baden, *("foule compacte s'amasse autour"),* Baudelaire's final moments in *Le Figaro* would seem to have been trivially obscured. And yet there is in this surprising journalistic coincidence of impressions—as Baudelaire remarked about the astonishing style of his mentor, Théophile Gautier—*"une justesse qui ravit"* ("an aptness that thrills").[2] For it was in the very pages of *Le Figaro*, some four years earlier that Baudelaire himself, in the context of his major essay on the art of modernity, had declared:

La femme . . . est surtout une harmonie générale . . . dans les mousselines, les gazes, les vastes et chatoyantes nuées d'étoffes dont elle s'enveloppe. . . . dans le métal et le minéral qui serpentent autour de ses bras et de son cou, qui ajoutent leurs étincelles aux feu de ses regards . . . Qui est l'homme qui . . . n'a pas joui, de la manière la plus désintéressée, d'une toilette savamment composée . . . ?

(Above all woman is a general harmony . . . in the muslins, the gauzes, the vast iridescent clouds of stuff in which she *envelops herself* . . . in the metal and mineral which twist and turn around her arms and neck, adding their sparks to the fire of her glance . . . Where is the man who . . . has not in the most disinterested of ways enjoyed a skillfully composed toilette?)[3]

In fact, as we know, what Baudelaire appreciated most about female appearance was precisely the extent to which it was adorned and embellished by the artful enhancements, the fantastic toilettes of fashion. Stripped bare of the refinements, the accessories, the sa-lutory—as opposed to dangerous—supplements of fashion, *"la femme est* naturelle, *c'est-à-dire, abominable"* ("woman is *natural,* that is to say, abominable").[4] In firm contradistinction to the "natural tastes" of a previous generation, for Baudelaire the state of "nature" or *"le naturel,"* morally connoted human depravity and evil; aesthetically it connoted the unsightly blemishes of a fallen world:

> *Tout ce que je dis de la nature comme mauvaise conseillère en matière de morale, et de la raison comme rédemptrice et réformatrice, peut être transporté dans l'ordre du beau. Je suis ainsi conduit à regarder la parure comme un des signes de la noblesse primitive de l'âme humaine.*

> (All that I am saying about Nature as a bad counsellor in moral matters, and about Reason as true redeemer and reformer, can be applied to the realm of beauty. I am thus led to regard external finery as one of the signs of the primitive nobility of the human soul.)

In the prose poem, *"L'Invitation au voyage,"* Baudelaire imagined the luxuriant paradise of this "primitive nobility": *"Pays singulier, supérieur aux autres, comme l'Art l'est à la Nature, où celle-ci est réformée par le rêve, où elle est corrigée, embellie, refondue"* (A singular land, superior to others, just as Art is to Nature; where Nature is reformed by dreams, where she is corrected, embellished, recast).[5] In *"Le peintre de la vie moderne,"* he admires, by extension, other "primitives" who intuit the moral and aesthetic principle of "Nature corrected by Art"; the "savage" and the child, for instance, who demonstrate *"la haute spiritualité de la toilette . . . par leurs aspirations naïves vers le brillant, vers les plumages bariolés, les étoffes chatoyantes, vers la majesté superlative des formes artificielles"* ("the lofty spiritual significance of the toilette . . . in their naive adoration of what is brilliant—many-colored feathers, iridescent fabrics, the incomparable majesty of artificial forms").

Fashion, the supplementary dazzle, color, and rustle of artifice that envelops the body—more specifically, the most "natural" and there-fore most disturbing of bodies, the female body—must be considered *"comme un symptôme du goût de l'idéal . . . comme un essai permanent et successif de réformation de la nature"* ("as a symptom of the taste for the ideal . . . as a permanent and repeated attempt at re-forming nature").[6]

In the passages that follow, Baudelaire focuses on the censured feminine practice of "maquillage" (putting on makeup), to defend and celebrate all the artful tactics by which material nature may be spir-itualized. Like his much-admired dandy whose only justification (and activity) is the fine grooming of his self-image, the woman who adorns herself proudly "makes herself up." Painted woman, but also painter, she invents beautiful illusions and thereby assumes the status of not just artist's model but model artist.

> *Ainsi, si je suis bien compris, la peinture du visage ne doit pas être employée dans le but vulgaire, inavouable, d'imiter la belle nature . . . Qui oserait assigner à l'art la fonction stérile d'imiter la nature? Le maquillage n'a pas à se cacher, à éviter de se laisser deviner; il peut au contraire, s'étaler . . . avec une espèce de candeur.*

> (Thus, if you will understand me aright, face painting should not be used with the vulgar, unavowable object of imitating Nature . . . *Who would dare assign to art the sterile function of imitating Nature?* Makeup has no need to hide itself or to shrink from being suspected; on the contrary, let it display itself . . . with frankness and honesty.)[7]

Nowhere is Baudelaire's aesthetic position on art and artifice made quite so explicitly, and nowhere do we recall more felicitously that in addition to theorizing about art, an *esthéticien* in French (or, *esthéticienne*) is also a beautician.

Baudelaire's "*Eloge du Maquillage,*" constitutes the eleventh chapter of "*Le Peintre de la vie moderne,*" an article in which the poet extols the example of Constantin Guys, an artist who, with a keen eye for fashion, paints modern women.

> *Si une mode, une coupe de vêtement a été légèrement transformée, si les noeuds de rubans, les boucles ont été détrônés par les cocardes, si le bavolet s'est élargi et si le chignon est descendu d'un cran sur la nuque . . . croyez qu'à une distance énorme son oeil d'aigle l'a déjà deviné. . . . Et les choses renaissent sur papier naturelles, et plus que naturelles, belles et plus que belles.*

> (If a fashion or the cut of a garment has been slightly modified, if bows and curls have been supplanted by cockades, if *bavolets* have been enlarged and *chignons* have dropped a fraction towards the nape of the neck. . . . be very sure that *his eagle eye* will already have spotted it . . . and the external world is reborn upon his paper, *natural and more than natural, beautiful and more than beautiful.*)[8]

The "*éloge du maquillage,*" coming as it does toward the end of this essay, thus offers us yet another example of what a different kind of modern artist might paint—her face, for instance. For the technical aspects of such painting, Baudelaire concentrates, as he does elsewhere in his art criticism, on the uses of line and color: white powder for the shoulders, rouge for the cheeks, and black liner for the eyes.

> . . . *qui ne voit [pas] que l'usage de la poudre de riz, si niaisement anathématisé par les philosophes candides, a pour but et pour résultat de faire disparaître du teint toutes les taches que la nature y a outrageusement semées, et de créer une unité abstraite dans le grain et la couleur de la peau, laquelle unité . . . rapproche immédiatement l'être humain de la statue, c'est-à-dire d'un être divin et supérieur? Quant au noir artificiel qui cerne l'oeil et au rouge qui marque la partie supérieure de la joue . . . ce cadre noir rend le regard plus profond et plus singulier, donne à l'oeil une apparence plus décidée de fenêtre ouverte sur l'infini; le rouge, qui enflamme la pommette, augmente encore la clarté de la prunelle et ajoute au beau visage féminin la passion mystérieuse de la prêtresse.*

> (. . . anyone can see that the use of rice powder, so stupidly anathematized by our Arcadian philosophers, is successfully designed to rid the complexion of those blemishes that Nature has outrageously strewn there, and thus to create an abstract unity in the color and the texture of the skin, a unity, which . . . immediately approximates the human being to the statue, that is, to something superior and divine. As for the artificial black with which the eye is outlined, and the rouge with which the upper part of the cheek is painted, . . . the black frame renders the glance more penetrating and individual and gives the eye a more decisive appearance of a window open upon the infinite; and the rouge which sets fire to the cheekbone only goes to increase the brightness of the pupil and adds to the face of a beautiful woman the mysterious passion of the priestess.)[9]

Framed by a discourse on painting and resonant with poetic overtones from *Les Fleurs du mal*, these have always struck me as extraordinary passages in Baudelaire's criticism—extraordinary for their striking metaphors, for their aesthetic (in both senses) insight, and for their unusual attention to the detail of a woman's toilette. In the context of the essay on Guys, it would be tempting to read these passages as representing Baudelaire's own eagle-eyed scrutiny of women in the streets of Paris and his curious arousal at the sight of their *"parure."* This passionate and intriguing discourse on fashion is mediated, however, by a close encounter of the textual—as opposed to sexual—kind: an encounter with the reflections of an artist for whom the *"superflu"* had long been declared *"nécessaire."* An author who had already devoted many pages of prose both to the nature of modern art and to the excitement of women's toilettes, and an author whom Baudelaire had already singled out as the "impeccable poet . . . master and friend," the "perfect magician of French letters," was Théophile Gautier.

In 1858, one year before Baudelaire began *"Le Peintre de la vie moderne,"* the editor Poulet-Malassis published a small pamphlet by Théophile Gautier, entitled *De la Mode.* The text of the pamphlet had originally appeared as an article in *L'Artiste* and had also appeared as a separate 12 page publication—printed on pink paper—that was sent as a bonus to subscribers of *Le Journal des Dames* and *Messager des Dames et des Demoiselles.*[10] The article, a defense of modern fashion, is directed to the many painters who refuse to paint their subjects in contemporary dress:

> *Statuaires et peintres se plaignent . . . Le costume moderne les empêche de faire des chefs-d'oeuvre; à les entendre, c'est la faute des habits noirs, des paletots et des crinolines s'il ne sont pas des Titien, des van Dyck, des Velasquez. Cependant ces grands hommes ont peint leurs contemporains dans des costumes . . . qui, parfois élégants, étaient souvent disgracieux ou bizarres. Notre costume est-il d'ailleurs si laid qu'on le prétend? N'a-t-il pas sa signification, peu comprise malheureusement des artistes tous imbus d'idées antiques?*

(Sculptors and painters complain . . . Modern dress has prevented them from making masterpieces; to listen to them, it's the fault of the black dress-coats, the topcoats and the crinolines that they are not Titians, Van Dycks or Velasquez. And yet, these great men painted their contemporaries in garb that . . . sometimes elegant, was often graceless or bizarre. Besides, is our dress in fact as ugly as they claim? Does it not possess its own significance, little understood, alas, by artists whose heads are filled with antique ideas?)[11]

The reference to the significance of *"notre costume"* and *"l'habit noir"* recalls the famous case that Baudelaire had made some twelve years earlier in the Salon of 1846 for the representation of contemporary dress in painting. *"Et cependant, n'a-t-il pas sa beauté et son charme indigène, cet habit tant victime?"* ("And all the same, has not this much-abused garb its own beauty and native charm?")[12] Gautier, however, extended his reflections beyond the black dress-coat to focus on the perceived extravagances of women's dress and toilette: crinolines and cosmetics. Within the context of his advice to painters he continues:

> *Avec le rare sentiment de l'harmonie qui les caractérise, les femmes ont compris qu'il y avait une sorte de dissonance entre la grande toilette et la figure naturelle. De même que les peintres habiles établissent l'accord des chairs et des draperies par des glacis légers, les femmes blanchissent leur peau qui paraîtrait bise à côté des moires, des dentelles, des satins, et lui donnent une unité de ton préférable à ces martelages de blanc, de jaune et de rose qu'offrent les teints les plus purs. Au moyen de cette fine poussière, elles font prendre à leur épiderme un mica de marbre, . . . La forme se rapproche ainsi de la statuaire; elle se spiritualise et se*

purifie. Parlerons-nous du noir des yeux, tant blâmé aussi: ces traits marqués
allongent les paupières, dessinent l'arc des sourcils, augmentent l'éclat des yeux,
et sont comme des coups de force que les maîtres donnent aux chefs-d'oeuvre
qu'ils finissent. La mode a raison sur tous les points.

(With that rare feeling for harmony that characterises them, women have
understood that there is a sort of dissonance between the grand toilette and
the *natural* face. Just as skillful painters establish a harmony between flesh
tones and draperies through the light application of a transparent coat of
color, women whiten their skin, which would otherwise appear swarthy
next to the moirés, the laces and the satins; they thus give it a unity of tone
that is preferable to those splashes of white, yellow and pink that mark
even the purest complexions. By means of this fine powder, their skin takes
on the sheen of a fine marble, . . . The [human] form thus approaches the
art of statuary; it becomes spiritualised and purified. We should speak of
the black eye makeup, that has also been much maligned: These drawn
lines lengthen the eyelid, define the arch of the brow, intensify the sparkle
of the eye and are like the deft strokes that a great painter gives to the
masterpiece he is just completing. In each instance, fashion proves correct.)[13]

Evidently Gautier had expanded his relation with Baudelaire from
poetic "mentor" to makeup consultant. In keeping with his many
literary reflections on the statuesque adornment of the female body,
Gautier clearly establishes here the significant link between *"les beaux-
arts"* and *"les arts de la beauté,"* between *"l'esthétique"* and *"l'esthétique."* Compared to the stodgy contemporary painters whom he invokes in his essay, the painted woman—that is, the painting woman—
is the superior artist of modern life. She has understood the laws of
color and of statuary, and used them toward the creation of a purer and
more spiritual beauty—referring all the while, through her fashionable dress, to her own ephemeral moment in time. She has revealed
that "eternal element" which constitutes one-half of the beautiful just
as she has reveled in the "relative, circumstantial element" that constitutes the other half. That second half, Baudelaire tells us, in his
famous definition of *"la beauté double,"* is *"tour à tour ou tout ensemble,*
l'époque, la mode, la morale, la passion. Sans ce second élément, qui est
comme l'enveloppe amusante, titillante . . . le premier élément serait . . .
inappréciable" ("whether severally or all at once, the age, its fashions,
its morals, its emotions. Without this second element, which might be
described as the amusing, enticing envelope . . . the first element
would be beyond our powers of appreciation").[14] As Gautier puts it,
rather more baldly, *"la mode a raison"* ("fashion proves correct").
Like Gautier, Baudelaire developed a discourse on fashion that was

founded on the language of painting and poetry. Hence, in his text, harmonies are achieved, beauty is spiritualized and *toilettes* are *savamment composées*. And what poet, he asks us, has not taken pleasure in reading the reasoned composition of a woman's toilette?

Which brings us back to the fantastic toilette of Cora Pearl, whose appearance at La Maison de Conversation provoked laughter and caused a riot as Baudelaire lay dying.[15] Just what was the meaning of that laughter?

Cora Pearl was one of the richest courtesans of the Second Empire; the source of her fortune was never a secret. An Englishwoman of lowly birth, she had slept her way through dukes and princes in the Imperial Court to the tune of 5,000 francs a night. When she briefly (and disastrously) appeared on stage in 1867 as Cupid in Offenbach's *Orphée aux Enfers,* she had her half-naked body covered in diamonds. With her ignoble origins and her utterly extravagant lifestyle, Cora appealed hugely to the Second Empire's fascination with vulgarity. But in a society that tried to mask its own parvenu origins and obsession with wealth behind pretenses to aristocratic distinction, the persona of Cora was also unmistakably embarrassing.

In a world full of people who had invented themselves, no one was more candid in "making herself up." "Cora Pearl" was herself a persona invented by the woman who proudly painted her—Emma Elizabeth Crouch of Devonshire. Elaborately "made up," she was known for changing the color of her hair, her carriage, and her servants' livery as the mood struck her. Happily departing from the natural look, for a while she created a vogue for pink hair. To be sure, in one version of her memoirs she takes full credit for having introduced the vogue for makeup in general during the Second Empire:

> It was about this time, . . . that I brought to Paris the habit of making up. Some of the ladies of the theatre had the habit of retaining their stage makeup during the late evening, but with ludicrous results, for their faces appeared pink and orange. . . . I had the idea that it should be possible to apply a lighter paint which would enhance the visage without making it ridiculous, and experimented at first alone, painting my face with tints of various colours, even including silver and pearl; I also used a dye from London to make my red hair yellow. When I first ventured forth after such an experiment, I was much admired; and soon after I had requests from other ladies to show them the art, . . .[16]

It was, however, in her toilettes, that Cora's art was most felt. Through the careful composition of her dress, she not only presented beautiful illusions, but also represented and exposed the charade of a bourgeois world that could not quite place her. In matters of fashion, she not only rivaled the styles of Paris' most respectable *grandes dames*, but, as she maintains, on occasion influenced them.

> My own style has altered from time to time. I certainly wore the cri-
> noline—indeed I was photographed in one of the widest in Paris, with
> twenty-four steels . . . but though it was said that the Empress herself
> dealt this fashion the deathblow in January of 1859, when she attended a
> court ball without a crinoline (a matter which took precedence in the
> newspapers even over Napoleon's New Year's speech to Baron Hübner!), I
> believe that I did as much as anyone else to end its predominance, drawing
> my dresses up over a petticoat and underskirts made of new stuffs and
> colors—a white dress over a lilac and black petticoat for instance. I also
> took to wearing tight sleeves and rich trimmings instead of flounces . . . It
> would be a mistake to believe that our influence upon fashion was exerted
> only at a distance; some of us were consistently seen in the best company.[17]

The artifices of fashion, like the artifices of makeup, may serve to embellish and ennoble an imperfect Nature. This is the aesthetic reading of fashion that Baudelaire provides; as such, the effects of fashion come to resemble the art of the poet who "molded mud into gold." Viewed from another perspective, however, that same art of fashion that so candidly presumes to challenge the natural order, also contains within it a disturbing, subversive quality that moralists of the time were quick to seize upon. Some, like the Procureur Général Dupin, in a speech delivered to the French Senate in 1865, "*Sur le luxe effréné des femmes,*" ("On Unrestrained Ostentation in Women") openly claimed that far from leading to art, effects of fashion lead straight to prostitution: "*N'est-ce pas une cause évidente de prostitution que l'exagération du luxe, que l'excès des toilettes, qui jettent tout le monde hors de ses voies?*" (Is it not an obvious cause of prostitution, this exaggerated display of luxury, the excesses of women's dress that throw everyone *off track*)[18]

Particularly dangerous for Dupin was the unnatural influence of high fashion on women of lower classes. "*Cela descend dans les classes inférieures par imitation, par esprit* d'égalité. *Chacune veut avoir la même toilette que les autres*" ("This trend has descended into the lower classes by imitation, by the spirit of *equality.* Every woman wants to have the same toilette as the others"). And here, indeed, fashion inspired Dupin to wax poetic:

> LaFontaine dans une de ces fables, se moque de la grenouille qui veut se faire
> aussi grosse qu'un boeuf; mais avec les modes d'aujourd'hui, la grenouille y
> parviendrait . . . (Hilarité générale. —Très-bien! Très-bien!)

(LaFontaine in one of his fables makes fun of a frog who wants to make itself as big as a bull; but with today's fashions [a reference to oversized crinolines], the frog would succeed . . . (General laughter. —Very good! Very good!)[19]

In addition to the little frogs that might dress like bulls, Dupin and his colleagues in the Senate had other things to worry about; as Cora herself asserted, some of their bullish wives were willingly fashioning themselves after rather impressive frogs.

On parle de courtisanes qui s'étalent dans les lieux publics. Oui, telle sera dans un équipage brillant, capable d'attirer les regards. Que fait la grande société? Elle regarde, elle prend modèle, et ce sont ces demoiselles qui donnent les modes même au dames du monde; ce sont elles qu'on copie, voilà l'exemple que donne la haute société.

(We have heard of courtesans who parade in public places. Yes, one such woman will be riding in a magnificent coach, drawing glances from everywhere. What does high society do? It looks on, it copies, and it is these *demoiselles* who dictate fashion even to society ladies; it is they who are copied. And this is the example that high society sets.)[20]

In short, the temptations of fashion implied not just the artful embellishment of nature, but moreover a threat to the very biology of society, capable of spawning mutant frogs and amphibious bulls.

During the Second Empire, only the wealthiest of women could afford to be outfitted by Charles Frederick Worth, the couturier to the Imperial Court. Worth provided court dresses and coronation clothes for Empresses and royalty throughout the world, but his fame was largely based on his responsibility for the gowns of the Empress Eugénie. And it was *chez* Worth, the court couturier, an expatriate Englishman himself, that Cora Pearl outfitted herself in the fantastic toilettes that became part of her legend. As fantastic as some of these toilettes must have looked, their appearance was still less outrageous than what they signified. For not only did Cora buy her dresses *chez* Worth, she ordered ivy-trimmed gowns (a preferred motif of the Empress) and ermine cloaks just to show that she could afford exactly the same clothes as Eugénie.

If the prostitute could dress like an empress, who then was to distinguish the empress from the prostitute? Eugénie Montijo, a Spaniard by birth, had, after all, risen to prominence through her affiliation with a wealthy and powerful man, and she was, in addition, a painted woman herself. Her heavy use of makeup long remained a subject of comment by ladies in the French court. As Maxime du Camp recalls:

Il y avait autour d'elle comme un nuage de cold-cream et de patchouli . . . les cheveux teints, le visage fardé, les yeux bordés de noir, les lèvres frottées de rouge, il lui manquait, pour être dans son vrai milieu, la musique du cirque olympique.

(There was about her something like a cloud of cold cream and patchouli oil . . . her hair dyed, her face all made up, her eyes lined in black, her lips colored red; the only thing missing, for her to be in her true milieu, was the music of the Olympic Circus.)[21]

In short, all made up and stepping out in her *toilette savamment composée*, Cora Pearl not only invented the poem of her own dazzling beauty, she also retold—artistically, ironically, menacingly perhaps—the fable of the Empress's new clothes.

And, as is the case of that story, the reactions to the story told by a toilette were inevitably bound up with nervous, uncomfortable laughter. A laughter with which Baudelaire could well identify. As he stated at the end of the *"Eloge du maquillage"*:

Je permets volontiers à ceux-là que leur lourde gravité empêche de chercher le beau jusque dans ses plus minutieuses manifestations, de rire de mes réflexions . . . leur jugement austère n'a rien qui me touche; je me contenterai d'en appeler auprès des véritables artistes ainsi que des femmes . . .

(I am perfectly happy for those whose ponderous gravity prevents them from seeking Beauty in its most minute manifestations to laugh at these reflections of mine . . . their austere verdict leaves me quite unmoved; I content myself with appealing to true artists as well as to women . . .)

No doubt Baudelaire would have enjoyed lying next to Cora in print.[22]

Notes

1. Jean Richer and Marcel Ruff, eds., *Les Derniers Mois de Charles Baudelaire*, (Paris: Nizet, 1976), 98. Unless otherwise indicated, all translations from the French are my own.

2. Charles Baudelaire, *Oeuvres complètes*, ed. Claude Pichois, 2 vols. (Paris: Gallimard, 1975), 2: 118. (Henceforth referred to as *OC*.)

3. *"Le Peintre de la vie moderne,"* *OC*, 2: 714. Trans. Jonathan Mayne, *The Painter of Modern Life and Other Essays*, (Oxford: Phaidon Press, 1965), 30–31. (My emphasis.) With minor adjustments, the translations from *"Le Peintre de la vie moderne"* all are taken from this edition.

4. "Mon coeur mis à nu," *OC*, 1: 677.

5. *OC*, 1: 302.

6. "Le Peintre de la vie moderne," *OC*, 2: 716.

7. Ibid., 717. (My emphasis.)

8. Ibid., 693–4. (Second emphasis mine.)

9. Ibid., 717.

10. Gautier, *De la Mode*, (Paris: Bonaventure et Ducessois, 1858).

11. Gautier, *De la Mode*, (Paris: Poulet-Malassis et De Broise, 1858), 10–11. (Henceforth referred to as *DM*.)

12. *OC*, 2: 494.

13. *DM*, 31–32.

14. *OC*, 2: 685.

15. During the Second Empire, Baden-Baden became the fashionable summer capital for *"le tout Paris."* The central meeting spot in the town was "La Maison de Conversation," known as the "Palais de Plaisir," a monumental neoclassical parody designed by Bénazet, a colonel in the Parisian national guard. In "Une Bonne Fortune," Musset provides the following amusing description:

> *Cette maison se trouve être un gros bloc fossile,*
> *Bâti de vive force à grands coups de moellon;*
> *C'est comme un temple grec, tout recouvert de tuile,*
> *Une espèce de grange avec un péristyle,*
> *Je ne sais quoi d'informe et n'ayant pas de nom,*
> *Comme un grenier à foin, bâtard du Panthéon.*

> (This house is something of a big fossil block,
> Forcefully built with great heaps of quarry stone;
> It is like a Greek temple, all covered with roof tiles,
> A kind of barn with a peristyle,
> A formless *je-ne-sais-quoi* that has no name,
> —A hay loft, bastard offspring of the Pantheon.)

On Baden-Baden, see Comte Fleury and Louis Sonolet, *La Société du Second Empire*, 4 vols. (Paris: Albin Michel, n.d.) 3: 433–40.

16. *The Memoirs of Cora Pearl*, ed. William Blatchford (London: Granada, 1983), 94–95. This edition of memoirs first appeared in 1890 in a collection of erotica. Unlike Cora Pearl's more polite, self-censored memoirs published by Jules Lévy in Paris in 1886, this version comes closer to the kind of explicitly sexual narrative one might have expected from the notorious courtesan. As William Blatchford, the editor of this version, indicates, the authenticity of the book's authorship may be questioned; it remains impossible to determine whether or not Cora Pearl actually penned these memoirs. Nevertheless, even if the memoirs were to be proved fictional, they still constitute a late nineteenth-century mythology of the infamous Cora.

17. Ibid., 96–97. On Cora Pearl and imperial society under Napoleon III, see S. C. Burchell, *Imperial Masquerade, The Paris of Napoleon III*, (New York: Atheneum, 1971), Joanna Richardson, *La Vie Parisienne 1852–1870*, (London: Hamish Hamilton, 1971), Albert D. Vandam, *Undercurrents of The Second Empire, Notes and Recollections*, (London: Heinemann, 1897) and Cora Pearl, *Mémoires de Cora Pearl*, (Paris: Jules Lévy, 1886).

18. In Jules Meugy, *L'Extinction de la Prostitution, Pétition au Sénat*, (Paris: Garnier, 1866), 70. (My emphasis.)

19. Ibid. In a passage that follows, Dupin, unwittingly perhaps, paraphrases the story of Emma Bovary:

> *Quand on va ou qu'on doit aller à une fête, qu'on veut y faire quelque figure, et qu'on n'a pas de quoi,*
> *l'amour-propre l'emporte, on répugne de le dire au mari, la caisse conjugale est vide; on s'habille au*

crédit, on signe des billets, des lettres de change, pour lesquelles on cherche des endosseurs, et dont l'échéance est toujours fatale à la vertu.

(When one goes or needs to go to a ball, and one wants to make an impression there, but one doesn't have the means, pride wins out; one is loath to tell one's husband, and so the household savings are liquidated; one buys dresses on credit, one signs banknotes and bills of exchange, for which one needs to find endorsers, bills which, when they come due, are always fatal to woman's virtue.)

20. Ibid., 69.

21. *Souvenirs d'un demi-siècle*, 2 vols. (Paris: Hachette, 1949) 1: 147. Cf. similar observations by the Princess Pauline von Metternich: *"Ce qui m'a surprise c'est que l'Impératrice peignait ses sourcils et les contours des yeux et cela très franchement avec de gros traits de crayon noir. J'ai appris plus tard, et cela par Elle-même, qu'elle avait pris cette habitude ayant en horreur les sourcils et cils blonds qui, disait-Elle: 'donnaient l'air bête et effacé'."* ("What surprised me was that the Empress outlined her eyebrows and the contour of her eyes most unsubtly with thick strokes of black pencil. I later learned from Her directly that she had taken up this habit because she detested blond lashes and brows which She claimed 'made one look stupid and washed-out'.") *Eclairs du passé (1859–1870)*, (Zurich: Amalthera Verlag, 1922), 199.

22. The relation between art and prostitution is a recurrent theme in Baudelaire's work. In the prose poem, *"Les Foules,"* Baudelaire describes the activity of the poet-*flâneur* as *"cette sainte prostitution de l'âme"* ("that holy prostitution of the soul"). Elsewhere, in his intimate journals he proclaims: *"Qu'est-ce que l'art? Prostitution"* ("What is art? Prostitution"). Baudelaire's identification with the prostitute is a complex one that extends well beyond the questions of fashion that are at issue in this study; it does, however, involve some measure of seduction and provocative self-display. On the poet as prostitute, see Leo Bersani, *Baudelaire and Freud*, (Berkeley: University of California Press, 1974).

Solipsism and Dialogue in Baudelaire's Prose Poems

EDWARD K. KAPLAN

The narrator's search for reciprocal communication, or dialogue, unifies Baudelaire's prose poem collection, posthumously entitled *Le Spleen de Paris. Petits Poëmes en prose*. My interpretation assumes its overall coherence and is confirmed by several factors, extrinsic as well as intrinsic to the ensemble of fifty. Most speculative is, perhaps, the fact that Baudelaire's autograph Table of Contents (Bibliothèque littéraire Jacques Doucet, Paris, MS 9022), on which the definitive edition (of 1869) was based, essentially preserves their prepublication order. Most of the previous sequences, especially the four groupings of twenty-six published or printed for *La Presse* in 1862, comprise its unchanging foundation. In terms of content, the narrator remains the same throughout. He is a self-critical *flâneur* who repeatedly attempts to reconcile his aesthetic and ethical drives; that is, he attempts to harmonize his solitary quest for perfect beauty with his desire to overcome social alienation.

The Parisian Prowler—as I entitle my translation of the "prose poems"—is not a random collection of lyrical tableaux, but rather "fables of modern life" which trace an itinerary.[1] Most of the pieces are allegorical or narrative, and not—according to stereotyped notions of the "prose poem"—lyrical, rhythmical, and picturesque. When they are, the aesthetic seduction is always compromised by some expression of ironic distance or commentary. Self-critical distance is, in fact, their distinctive mark: A skeptical reader gradually emerges from within the texts to question the literary endeavor itself.

The first two fables compose a diptych which introduces thematically the entire adventure: *"L'Etranger"* and *"Le désespoir de la vieille,"* initiate the struggle between solipsism and dialogue. The "aesthetic stranger" of fable no. 1 claims *"Je n'ai ni père, ni mère, ni soeur, ni frère"* ("I have neither father, nor mother, nor sister, nor brother"). When asked about his homeland, *"Ta patrie?"* he answers *"J'ignore sous quelle latitude elle est située"* ("Your fatherland?" "I am unaware in what latitude it lies"). He commits himself only to constant imaginative mobility. At the end of the abortive dialogue he literally spaces out: *"J'aime les nuages . . . les nuages qui passent . . . là-bas . . . là-bas . . . les merveilleux nuages!"* ("I love clouds . . . drifting clouds . . . there . . . over there . . . marvelous clouds!"). The suspension points reinforce the testimony that his life's emptiness impels him to project his denied yearnings endlessly.

The old woman of the next fable—the collection's "ethical stranger"—fails to arouse a sympathetic response from an infant. The "innocent" child is afraid of her wrinkled face: *"Alors la bonne vieille se retira dans sa solitude éternelle. . . ."* ("Then the kind old woman withdrew into her eternal solitude"). Like her male counterpart, she remains emprisoned within her fantasy, but unlike him, she deplores her condition. The forty-eight fables that follow are unified by similar struggles to reconcile essential solitude with a reciprocal, social existence.

Aesthetic Solipsism

The collection's dominant strand develops the "aesthetic" utopia of solipsism, the "artist's" solution to life's obstacles and imperfections.[2] The reality inside the mind appears to be more real than the world outside. The "aesthetic" narrator (usually considered to be Baudelaire's only authentic proxy) is an unemployed writer and observer of urban mores who seeks material for his fiction, or, failing that, to mold fantasy into a way of life. But his "homes" are usually antagonistically dual, conveying the fragility of imagination. Many of the pieces describe his rooms which, like *"La Chambre double"* ("The double room," no. 5), collapse the dreamed world: *"Et ce parfum d'un autre monde, dont je m'enivrais avec une sensibilité perfectionnée, hélas, il est remplacé par une fétide odeur de tabac mêlée à je ne sais quelle moisissure"* ("And that scent of another world, which I used to intoxicate myself with a perfected sensibility, alas! It was replaced by a fetid odor of tobacco mixed with some sort of nauseating mustiness"). The chamber of poverty on the *sixième*, where the narrator of *"Le Mauvais Vitrier"* ("The bad glazier," no. 9) lives, is all too real; and so he attacks the honest glazier for not literalizing a cliché which signifies the denial of reality: *"Comment? vous n'avez pas de verres de couleur? des verres roses, rouges, bleus, des vitres magiques, des vitres de paradis? Impudent que vous êtes! vous osez vous promener dans des quartiers pauvres, et vous n'avez pas même des vitres qui fassent voir la vie en beau!"* ("What? You have no colored panes? No pink panes, no red, no blue, no magic panes, no panes of paradise? You are shameless! You dare walk through poor neighborhoods, and you don't even have panes which make life beautiful!")

Even in the double-locked room of *"A Une heure du matin"* ("At one o'clock in the morning," no. 10), the writer cannot enjoy his *"bain de ténèbres"* ("bath of darkness"). He never remains free from the "tyranny of the human face," the other, the proxy of his social condition and its responsibilities.

Baudelaire's interpreters tend to accept his escapism as completely in earnest. Barbara Johnson was perhaps the first to emphasize the self-critical foundation of such patently "poetic" pieces as *"Un hémisphère dans une chevelure"* and *"L'invitation au voyage"* ("A hemisphere in tresses," "Invitation to the voyage," nos. 17–18), which undermine their own lyricism, as well as putting into question their verse "doublets" from *Les Fleurs du Mal*.[3] The essential innovation of Baudelaire's modern fables is precisely their systematic self-criticism—to the point of formulating a question of reality which challenges all literary utopias. *"Les projets"* ("Plans," no. 24) formulates the clearest, and perhaps the most radical position. Once again, the problem is one of solitude. The story begins with a reflexive verb *"Il se disait"* ("He was saying to himself"), as the narrator engages in an admittedly monological stroll, reflecting constantly upon himself, and erecting a series of ideal worlds. And finally, as a conclusion, he states this rhetorical challenge: *"J'ai eu aujourd'hui, en rêve, trois domiciles où j'ai trouvé un égal plaisir. Pourquoi contraindre mon corps à changer de place, puisque mon âme voyage si lestement? Et à quoi bon exécuter des projets, puisque le projet est en lui-même une jouissance suffisante?"* ("Today, in dream, I had three domiciles where I found equal pleasure. Why force my body to change location, when my soul travels so nimbly? And what good is it to carry out plans, since planning itself is a sufficient delight?")

An unironic reading of this question implies, of course, that fantasy is indeed enough. Other fables reinforce this positive solipsism, particularly the three most celebrated imaginative manifestos. *"Enivrez-vous"* ("Get high," no. 33) which proclaims: *"Il faut être toujours ivre. Tout est là: c'est l'unique question"* ("You must always get high. Everything depends upon it: It is the only question"). The putative equivalence of "wine, poetry, or virtue" as sources of this "inspiration" undermines this advice with an irony perceptible only to readers who—encouraged by other self-questioning fables—sympathetically cleave to the reality principle.

"Les fenêtres" ("Windows," no. 35), and the antepenultimate, "Any where out of the world" (*"N'importe où hors du monde,"* no. 48) also

appear to promote escape above all. But they also broadcast their substratum of anguish—though, at the same time, they claim that anguish is artistically useful. More significantly, these aesthetic fantasies have a Socratic function: They simultaneously celebrate forms of inspiration which may produce works of art while demonstrating that imaginative self-intoxication is primarily an escape from normal everyday demands for reciprocal communication, responsible choices, and action. The vaunted "freedom" of the "aesthetic" cannot leave the dreamer's head.

"*Enivrez-vous,*" the prototypical manifesto, is most explicit: "*Pour n'être pas les esclaves martyrisés du Temps, enivrez-vous sans cesse*" ("So as not to be the martyred slaves of Time, get high; get high constantly!"). "*Les fenêtres*" (no. 35)—elegantly analyzed by Sima Godfrey—reformulates the fundamental question which preceding aesthetic fables had not entirely hidden, but as well had not thematized as dramatically.[4] After imagining the "legend" of a poor, older woman whom he studies through a closed window, the narrator ends with a bold defense of inspiration as conveying essential being. He formulates an ontological question, but this time, with an extraordinary innovation in his narrative; he exteriorizes his own self-questioning through a skeptical reader who steps directly from the outside world into the text:

> *Peut-être me direz-vous: "Es-tu sur que cette légende soit la vraie?" Qu'importe ce que peut être la réalité placée hors de moi, si elle m'a aidé à sentir que je suis et ce que je suis?* (italicized in Baudelaire's manuscript)

> ("Perhaps you will ask, 'Are you sure that legend is the true one?' Does it matter what the reality located outside of me might be, if it has helped me to live, to feel that I am and *what* I am?")

The narrator's rhetorical answer appears to assert his writing principle over his reality principle, but it can also imply the opposite response. *What* he is is an author; *who* he is is a person in the world. This ontological question reiterates the solipsistic challenge at the end of "*Les projets*" (Plans). Can the artist's being truly depend upon untruth? Or on self-delusion? Readers must choose some sort of answer, accepting the narrator's boldly stated solipsism or siding with his lucid acknowledgement of reality. Or, of course, the choice can remain undecided.

The antepenultimate fable begins and ends with an internal dialogue between the narrator and his mind (or soul). "*N'importe où hors du monde*" ("Anywhere out of the world") summarizes all attempts to find stability beyond the world as it exists, as the title suggests in two languages. The chronically dissatisfied idealist seeks a home: *"Dis-moi, mon âme, pauvre âme refroidie, que penserais-tu d'habiter Lisbonne?"* ("Tell me, my soul, my poor benumbed soul, what would you think about residing in Lisbon?"). No answer. *"Puisque tu aimes tant le repos, avec le spectacle du mouvement, veux-tu venir habiter la Hollande, cette terre béatifiante?"* ("Since you love calm so much, added to the view of movement, do you want to come reside in Holland, that beatifying land?"). The dreamer's spirit (or imagination) proves to be irremediably restless, pointing only to the ultimate solution, the cure for all dissatisfaction: *"S'il en est ainsi, fuyons vers les pays qui sont les analogies de la Mort"* ("So you have reached that degree of stupor where you can take pleasure only in your affliction? If it is thus, let's flee toward the countries which are the analogies of Death"). Ultimately, poetic idealism is suicide. The search for perfect "pleasure" (sensations or fantasy) has no dialogical application.

Ethical Reciprocity

The strand of "ethical fables" puts into an even more critical perspective the strand of "aesthetic fables," such as the ones just examined. I consider these "ethical fables" to be fundamental to Baudelaire's new genre, and in fact more significant than his aesthetic idealizations, since their primary function is to undermine verbal or fantasied transcendence of otherness. "Dialogue" now emerges as the narrator's primary goal, thus extending into narrative or parabolic form the embrace of finitude expressed in poems he added to the 1861 revision of *Les Fleurs du Mal,* such as *"Le Masque"* (no. 20 in *Spleen et Idéal*) in which the poet-narrator denounces the "blasphemy of art"— both because it is untruth (an ontological issue) and, ethically, because it denies the fellowship of human fallibility.[5] The section *Tableaux parisiens* represents the fullest development of Baudelaire's embrace of an aesthetics of finitude.

Baudelaire's ethical fables depict the narrator overcoming his detachment and identifying with another person, male or female, who has found a companion to his or to her solitude. The most dramatic of these is *"Les Veuves"* (Widows, no. 13) whose lyrical ending celebrates the poet's inspiration, as it arises from his compassion for the woman and her child, a little boy; the process generates verse before our eyes. *"Les Veuves"* is the only fable in the entire collection which ends with an alexandrine, and it is preceded by three lines of six syllables each, when pronounced normally (my quotation separates the last lines):

Et elle sera rentrée à pied, méditant et rêvant, seule, toujours seule; car l'enfant
est turbulent, égoïste, sans douceur et sans patience;
et il ne peut même pas,
comme le pur animal,
comme le chien et le chat,
servir de confident aux douleurs solitaires.

("And she probably walked home, meditating and dreaming, alone, forever alone. For a child is unruly, selfish, without gentleness and without
patience; and he cannot even, like a mere animal, like a dog or a cat, serve
as a confidant to lonely sorrows.")

The *flâneur* has identified with both the widow and (especially, I would
say) her little boy. The blank verse conveying his pathos emerges from
the typographical format of the prose to consecrate the narrator's
implicit identity as a poet-widowed mother, a lonely Parisian poet,
made fertile through compassion and love.

The next momentous identification occurs in *"Les Vocations"*
("Vocations," no. 31), which recapitulates many of the "Parisian
prowler's" aesthetic paradises. Here, four boys discuss their
dissatisfaction at home and their various solutions to ennui. The
fourth boy summarizes his friends' quests and then asserts his own; he
seems to be a preadolescent version of the "stranger" of fable no. 1, or
the little boy of *"Les Veuves"* ("Widows," no. 13), a few years older
and anticipating his independence. (I don't consider the reversal of
numbers 13/31 to be significant, but worth mentioning for those who
do.) This boy anticipates the escapist of fable no. 48:

"Vous savez que je ne m'amuse guère à la maison; on ne me mène jamais au
spectacle; mon tuteur est trop avare; Dieu ne s'occupe pas de moi et de mon
ennui, et je n'ai pas une belle bonne pour me dorloter. Il m'a souvent semblé que
mon plaisir serait d'aller toujours droit devant moi, sans savoir où, sans que
personne s'en inquiète, et de voir toujours des pays nouveaux. Je ne suis jamais
bien nulle part, et je crois toujours que je serais mieux ailleurs que là où je suis."

("You know that I have hardly any fun at home; I'm never taken to plays;
my guardian is too stingy; God doesn't bother with me and my ennui, and
I don't have a beautiful maid to coddle me. I've often thought that my
pleasure would be to travel continuously straight ahead, without knowing
where, without anyone bothering me, and always to see new lands. I'm
never at ease anywhere, and I always believe I'd feel better anywhere else
than where I am.")

So this fourth boy follows three gypsy musicians, until, inhibited as were the others, he stops, afraid to leave France. Now the narrator, right before the epilogue, intervenes:

> *L'air peu intéressé des trois autres camarades me donna à penser que ce petit était déjà un* incompris [Baudelaire's emphasis]. *Je le regardais attentivement; il y avait dans son oeil et dans son front ce je ne sais quoi de précocement fatal qui éloigne généralement la sympathie, et qui, je ne sais pourquoi, excitait la mienne, au point que j'eus l'idée bizarre que je pouvais avoir un frère à moi-même inconnu.*

("The uninterested attitude of the other three friends made me reflect that this little one was already one of the *misunderstood*. I examined him carefully. There was something or other precociously fatal in his eyes and on his brow which generally repels sympathy, and which, I don't know why, aroused mine, so that for an instant I had the weird thought that I might have a brother to me unknown.")

This *explicit* assertion of brotherhood allows us to translate some of the more ambiguous expressions of ethical communion.[6] In each case, the narrator appears to insist upon his *inability* to act upon his compassion. This occurs, first, in *"Le Vieux saltimbanque"* ("The old acrobat," no. 14) that directly follows *"Les Veuves."* Here the narrator encounters "the ruin of a man," an old clown who represents, as he says all too baldly, *"l'image du vieil homme de lettres qui a survécu à la génération dont il fut le brillant amuseur; du vieux poète sans amis, sans famille, sans enfants, dégradé par sa misère et par l'ingratitude publique, et dans la baraque de qui le monde oublieux ne veut plus entrer!"* ("the image of the old writer who has survived the generation whose brilliant entertainer he was; of the old poet without friends, without family, without children, debased by his wretchedness and the public's ingratitude, and whose booth the forgetful public no longer wants to enter!"). There exists in Baudelaire's work no more forceful figuration of himself as an isolated, childless bachelor, without family or friends or lover.[7]

More significant, however, is the narrator's unsuccessful attempt to complete a charitable act after experiencing an emotional paralysis. He simply cannot ex-press his tears, his pity: *"Je sentis ma gorge serrée par la main terrible de l'hystérie, et il me sembla que mes regards étaient offusqués par ces larmes rebelles qui ne veulent pas tomber"* ("I felt my throat strangled by the dreadful hand of hysteria, and my sight seemed to be blocked by rebellious tears refusing to fall").

Similarly, the narrator of *"Une Mort héroïque"* ("A Heroic Death," no. 27), is paralyzed by his surfeit of feeling, this time, as a writer: *"Ma plume tremble, et des larmes d'une émotion toujours présente me montent aux yeux pendant que je cherche à vous décrire cette inoubliable soirée. Fancioulle me prouvait, d'une manière péremptoire, irréfutable, que l'ivresse de l'Art est plus apte que toute autre à voiler les terreurs du gouffre . . ."* ("My pen trembles, and tears of a still-present emotion fill my eyes as I try to describe that unforgettable evening. Fancioulle proved to me, in a peremptory, irrefutable way, that the intoxication of Art is more fit than any other to veil the terrors of the abyss"). The narrator has made some progress; he can weep, but he cannot write. In both cases, he fails to complete the dialogical contact with the afflicted artist, his unknown brother. It appears that Baudelaire's fables—both the aesthetic and the ethical ones—decisively reject the possibility of reciprocal communication. The narrator seeks dialogue, but his own reaching toward the other remains blocked. But can the writer ever reconcile his compassion with his drive to create and to dream? Can his inner and outer "rooms" ever become one? Where can he live? Can literature provide such a haven?

A Dialogical Conclusion

In the light of these, and several other fables, depicting essential solitude, *"Les Bons Chiens"* ("The Good Dogs," no. 50), the final piece, lyrically and unironically celebrates the writer's successful dialogue. Many astute readers have resisted the fable's lyricism (most obviously conveyed by the repeated refrains) and simplicity, considering it as too atypical of *Le Spleen de Paris* or even as a "mere literary exercise." Quite the contrary, I consider *"Les Bons Chiens"* as the appropriate confirmation of *"Le Thyrse"* ("The Thyrsus," no. 32), and *"Un cheval de race"* ("A Thoroughbred," no. 39), and *"Mademoiselle Bistouri"* ("Miss Scalpel," no. 47) which, without irony, embrace time and its travails. This final piece allows us to translate the implicit expressions of brotherhood submerged in the irony of other pieces. Furthermore, *"Les Bons Chiens"* was dedicated with utter sincerity to the animal painter, Joseph Stevens, as *"Le Thyrse"* was to Franz Liszt—unlike his dedication of the *La Presse* sequence to its artistic editor Arsène Houssaye.[8] *"Les Bons Chiens,"* therefore, stands as a fit conclusion to the completed collection of fifty.

Some knowledge of the biographical circumstances of its composition reinforces our analysis of its structural prominence. In 1865, two years before his death, Baudelaire, his nervous system and morale undermined by a previously dormant syphilitic infection, unable to sell his literary capital in Paris, fled his creditors to Belgium, where he gave several unsuccessful lectures. He increasingly dreaded mental and physical collapse. Among the rare friends who alleviated the anguish of his exile were the Stevens brothers, the art dealer Arthur, and the painters Alfred and Joseph. And, although Baudelaire complained about it, *"Les Bons Chiens"* was published three times before he placed it on his written Table of Contents as the fiftieth, and culminating, piece.

The narrator summarizes in "doggy language" (to use Michael Riffaterre's useful notion of "descriptive code") all the previous avatars of his solitude, alienation, and aspirations:

> *"Je chante le chien crotté, le chien sans domicile, le chien flâneur, le chien saltimbanque, le chien dont l'instinct, comme celui du pauvre, du bohémien et de l'histrion, est merveilleusement aiguillonné par la nécessité, cette si bonne mère, cette vraie patronne des intelligences.*

> ("I sing the muddied dog, the poor dog, the homeless dog, the stroller dog, the acrobat dog, the dog whose instinct, like that of the poor, of gypsies and actors, is marvelously goaded by necessity, such a good mother, true patroness of minds!")

"The muddied dog," too poor to rent a carriage, had appeared as the glazier (fable no. 9), the struggling writer (no. 10), and the many impoverished people who populate *The Parisian Prowler* (nos. 2, 13, 15, 19, 26, 28, 30, 35, 49). "The homeless dog" summarizes the solitary strangers (nos. 1, 2, 23), gypsies and wanderers (nos. 6, 24, 31, 41, 48), and the city's ambulatory schizophrenics (nos. 22, 47). "The stroller dog" reinacts the narrator's various walks, travels, thoughts, and invented legends, while "the acrobat dog" remains the traditional Romantic personification of the artist (nos. 3, 7, 14, 20, 21, 31, 36).

It is an appropriate irony, though bitter to contemplate, that the narrator, like the author, had found effective friendship only in his Belgian exile. Like the family of Victor Hugo with whom he also became close, he discovered a community like the gypsies of *"Les Vocations"* (no. 31) who quite happily lived "no where" *(nulle part).* The successful "exchange" of an inspirational vest reconciles the "ethical" and "aesthetic" dimensions of his inspiration:

> *Aucun de ceux qui étaient présents dans la taverne de la rue Villa-Hermosa n'oubliera avec quelle pétulance le peintre s'est dépouillé de son gilet en faveur du poète, tant il a bien compris qu'il était bon de chanter les pauvres chiens.*

> ("None of those present in the tavern on the Villa-Heromosa will forget how impetuously the painter shed his vest on behalf of the poet, so keenly did he recognize how good and honorable it was to sing of pitiful dogs.")

The narrator, "the poet," now steps out of literature, but through literature, as he responds to "the painter's" concrete gift. *"Les Bons Chiens,"* the prose poem itself, is both a parable and a product of friendship fulfilled. The final paragraph returns to a more habitual form of "poetic" prose; closing the collection, it repeats the refrain which condenses the narrator's deepest resource, both intimate and artistic: *Et toutes les fois que le poète endosse le gilet du peintre, il est contraint de penser aux bon chiens, aux chiens philosophes, aux été de la Saint Martin et à la beauté des femmes très-mûres.* ("And every time the poet dons the painter's vest, he is compelled to think of good dogs, of philosophical dogs, of Indian summers, and of the beauty of women quite mature.")

This culminating refrain highlights the ethical energy of the narrator's inspiration, while it ends his journey with the superlative *"des femmes très-mûres"* ("women quite mature"). Images of transition combine, like the widowed mother, the middle-aged woman of *"Un cheval de race"* ("A Thoroughbred," no. 39), and *"Mlle. Bistouri"* ("Miss Scalpel," no. 47), erotic sensuousness, emotional ripeness, anticipatory grief, and persistently passionate hope. Women who have endured life—like the woman under the mask in poem no. 20 of the 1861 *Fleurs de Mal*—reflect the narrator's adherence to shared reality.

Perhaps the Parisian Prowler has found someone he can love. Or perhaps he has simply created another "legend" disguised as compassionate empathy. Baudelaire the essayist was quite aware that aesthetic projection and ethical sensitivity can never be entirely separated.[9] Yet, the ending of his remarkable fables of modern life ratifies his fundamentally ethical stance. Experienced women, lovely women "past their prime" (see no. 27, "The Temptations")—not perfect, youthful, idealized, and sexually terrifying women—conquer Time with their enduring love. Whether or not they represent his mother or simply a contemporary of the forty-five-year-old poet, the final word *"très-mûre,"* makes of mortality—acceptance of the real and its intrinsic beauty—the seal of his wisdom and his art.

Notes

1. All quotations are taken from Baudelaire, *Oeuvres complètes*, Vol. 1, ed. Claude Pichois (Paris: Gallimard, Editions de la Pléiade, 1975) and the translations from Ch. Baudelaire, *The Parisian Prowler*, trans. Edward K. Kaplan (Athens and London: The University of Georgia Press, 1989). The ideas sketched in this paper are developed within the full context of the collection in my book, *Baudelaire's Prose Poems: The Esthetic, the Ethical, and the Religious in "The Parisian Prowler"* (The University of Georgia Press, 1990).

2. A team of researchers under the direction of Lucien Goldmann has defined these

thematic "strands": See Agnes Krutwig Caers, "La vision du monde dans les *Petits Poëmes en prose*," *Revue de l'Institut de Sociologie* 3–4 (1973): 625–39.

3. See Barbara Johnson's doctoral thesis, *Défigurations du langage poétique. La seconde révolution baudelairienne* (Paris: Flammarion, 1979), and revised chapters published in *The Critical Difference* (Baltimore: The Johns Hopkins University Press, 1980) and *A World of Difference* (The Johns Hopkins University Press, 1987).

4. Sima Godfrey, "Baudelaire's Windows," *L'Esprit Créateur* 22, 4 (Winter 1982): 83–100.

5. See Edward K. Kaplan, "Modern French Poetry and Sanctification: Charles Baudelaire and Yves Bonnefoy," *Dalhousie French Studies* 8 (Spring-Summer 1985), 103–25.

6. The fourth boy recalls Baudelaire's portrait of Edgar Allan Poe with whom he also identified: cf. Baudelaire, *Oeuvres complètes*, vol. 2 (Editions de la Pléiade, 1976), 269.

7. See Charles Mauron's analysis of Baudelaire's "superimposed" images of the widow and the old acrobat, *Le Dernier Baudelaire* (Paris: Corti, 1966), 49–55, and my article, "Baudelaire's Portrait of the Poet as Widow," *Symposium* 34, 3 (Fall 1980): 233–48.

8. See Ross Chambers, "Baudelaire et la pratique de la dédicace," *Saggi e ricerche di letteratura francese* 24 (1985): 121–40.

9. Baudelaire stated that aesthetic pleasures might easily become confused with ethical sensitivity: *"Le goût de la protection, un sentiment de paternité ardente et dévouée peuvent se mêler à une sensualité coupable que le haschisch saura toujours excuser et absoudre"* ("The liking for protection, fervent and devoted paternal feelings can be mixed in with a culpable sensuality of which hashish can always absolve us"), in *Le Poëme du hachisch* (1858), Baudelaire, *Oeuvres complètes*, vol. 1, 433.

You Cannot Kill a Cloud: Code and Context in "L'Etranger"

PETER SCHOFER

"A context is potentially unfinalized; a code must be finalized. A code is only a technical means of transmitting information, but it also has cognitive, creative significance. A code is a deliberately established, killed context." M. M. Bakhtin[1]

Bakhtin's assertion that context and code maintain an oppositional relationship provides a fruitful entry into Baudelaire's *Le Spleen de Paris*. Baudelaire's famous declaration that the various prose poems can be cut off from one another and that the fragments can *"exister à part"* ("exist separately") immediately warns us that context in the prose poems is not of a conventional sort and that it is not at all "finalized." Rather, the texts in Baudelaire's work resemble more closely a continuously shuffled deck of cards, where, with each shuffle, a new set of contexts is created. The context is not limited—finalized—by the relationships within the work itself. Here Bakhtin's open notion of context is taken in its literal and broadest sense: On the formal level, the context includes the dialogic relationship of one specific text to other texts or utterances, whether they be in the same work or part of a larger group of literary traces or threads. Thematically, the context can weave an almost infinite pattern of associations or "responses" on the social, political, philosophical, or cultural level, with references outside the text under study. The title, *Le Spleen de Paris*, opens up such contextual avenues. First, and most obvious, of course, are references to *Les Fleurs du mal*, through the word "spleen." As many critics have noted, the highlighting of Paris suggests a larger series of contexts—cultural, economic, social, and political. While the actual context "Paris" is finite, the possible combinations transcend the imagination. Critics as diverse as Suzanne Bernard and Barbara Johnson have emphasized that Baudelaire's prose poems do not adhere to traditional literary codes and they defy classification, or encoding.[2]

The first prose poem in the collection, "L'Etranger," is emblematic of the elusive relationship between context and code in the entire work:

Qui aimes-tu le mieux, homme énigmatique, dis? ton père, ta mère, ta soeur ou ton frère?
Je n'ai ni père, ni mère, ni soeur, ni frère.
Tes amis?
Vous vous servez là d'une parole dont le sens m'est resté jusqu'à ce jour inconnu.
Ta patrie?
J'ignore sous quelle latitude elle est située.
La beauté?
Je l'aimerais volontiers, déesse et immortelle.
L'or?
Je le hais comme vous haïssez Dieu.
Eh! qu'aimes-tu donc, extraordinaire étranger?
J'aime les nuages . . . les nuages qui passent . . . là-bas . . . là bas . . . les merveilleux nuages.

("Whom do you love most, enigmatic man, say? Your father, your mother, your sister, or your brother? / I have neither father, mother, sister, or brother. / Your friends? / You use a word there whose meaning has remained unknown to me until this day. / Your country [fatherland]? / I do not know on what latitude it is located. / Beauty? / I would love it, goddess and immortal. / Gold? / I hate it as you hate God. / Well! what do you love, extraordinary stranger? / I love the clouds . . . the clouds that pass . . . over there . . . over there . . . the marvelous clouds.")

The title *"etranger,"* suggests a code for reading the text, based on the meanings of foreigner, stranger, or alien. A traditional reading would concentrate on the personage of the stranger and his replies as a means to decode the text. However, the first marker after the title is not that of the *étranger,* but rather of the equally enigmatic interlocutor whose utterance *"Qui aimes-tu le mieux, homme énigmatique, dis?"* ("Whom do you love most, enigmatic man, say?") introduces his search for knowledge and an attempt to "decode" the alien. In some respects, the reader and the interlocutor are on the same level, both trying to understand the "other." However, if the reader limits reading the text by identifying with the interlocutor, a misleading and partial decoding results, since the interlocutor will remain a sort of transparent conduit for the reader's attempt at interpretation. A reading of the text *étranger,* not the person *étranger,* demands that the discourse of the interlocutor be taken into consideration. Thus, at the outset, an eccentric reading, one which is off center, which places emphasis on the interlocutor, will show how Baudelaire creates contexts without directly saying so and how he pits context against attempts to impose codes and to decode. A traditional reading concentrates on the foreigner and his series of enigmatic replies to very specific questions. The replies culminate in the ambiguous assertion that he loves *"les nuages . . . les nuages qui passent . . . là-bas . . . là-bas"* ("the clouds . . . the clouds which pass . . . down there . . . down there"). He gives us little substance, only movement, distance and objects which shift and change their form.

But substance is out there, in the form of the interlocutor, the very antithesis of the strange lover of clouds. His very first question reveals much about his character and opens us to Baudelaire's context: *"Qui aimes-tu le mieux homme énigmatique, dis? Ton père, ta mère, ta soeur, ou ton frère?"* He is aggressively, even rudely and crudely seeking knowledge, but his starting point, the family, assumes that the foreigner is like everyone else. In a number of ways, the questioner is trying to impose a way of thinking on the victim, not only in his priorities of family, then friends, and then country, but also in his paradoxical approach: On the one hand he shows ignorance by calling the foreigner "enigmatic." Yet in categorizing or labeling the stranger as enigmatic, he assumes previous knowledge of the man, as though he were in the middle of an ongoing conversation to which the reader was not privy. At the same time, he uses the *"tu"* form of address, thus asserting a familiarity or superiority over his interlocutor. While his aggressive interrogation nets him no information except negations and ambiguities, he insists on asking more questions which reveal more about himself than about the alien. We learn that he values the family first and even has in mind an ideal family of five members. His questions then enlarge the scope of values to include friends and patriotism (note that he says *"patrie"* [fatherland], not *"pays"* [country]).

The next two questions would appear to propose contrasting absolute values, beauty and gold, but they are not necessarily contradictory in a society where gold can buy beauty and where beauty has its price. However they can be looked on as two poles or extremes in sets of values that the interlocutor is using in the hope of drawing out the alien and getting a reply. In all the questions, he expects clear, precise, direct replies to his clear, precise, direct questions. But often the precise questions are almost impossible to answer. For example, can one honestly state which member of the family one loves most? Above all, he seeks knowledge which will permit him to classify and categorize the unknown figure. By his choice of questions, he needs to know, he needs to categorize, and he seeks to define. But all of these typically bourgeois traits result in a failure. Contextually, the inter-locutor stands almost as a stereotype or even a caricature of the nineteenth-century Parisian bourgeois, but by the nature of his ques-tions he does not specify what group he comes from. He could easily be a banker, an industrialist, a doctor, a psychologist, or even a police inspector. But the type of person is not as important as the type of discourse which he uses. It is interesting to note, for example, that one assumes that the interlocutor is a man, not a woman. His is a discourse which prevailed when Baudelaire was writing, at a time when there was an almost obsessional need to order and to classify.[3] We can go so far as to say that he is a proprietor by the way in which he seeks to appropriate speech.[4] Through controlling speech, he can appropriate the other person, and, in a sense, own him. But he meets in defeat in his attempt to acquire more, and his epistemological framework is shattered. He begins assertively, suggesting strongly that through direct questioning evidence can be uncovered. He is especially con-fident and presumptuous by asking very personal questions about love and family. The search for truth knows no codes of politeness or delicacy. He is also undaunted by potential contradictions: Even though he knows that the stranger is enigmatic (i.e., a riddle or someone speaking in riddles), he is confident that he can cut through the riddles and discover truth. Perhaps the two most important words of his text are the exclamation *"Eh!"* and the word *"étranger,"* in his final question, when he gives up. With the exclamatory *"Eh!,"* he momentarily recognizes defeat of his system and the triumph of the stranger's system of knowledge. He is nearly speechless and can use only a minimal code to express himself. However, by labelling his adversary an *"étranger"* he can claim a partial victory. Finally, he has found a label, one which reestablishes the validity of his own way of thinking and satisfies his need to label and to classify. He literally alienates the stranger, as he casts him out of his own epistemological sphere, where the alien presents no threat. In a slightly different context, Foucault has written that

> . . . *l'aliénation désigne au contraire une prise de conscience par laquelle le fou est reconnu, par sa société, comme étranger à sa propre patrie; on ne le libère pas de sa responsabilité, on lui assigne, au moins sous la forme de parenté et de voisinages complices, une culpabilité morale; on le désigne comme l'Autre, comme l'Etranger, comme l'Exclu.*[5]

(. . . on the contrary, alienation designates a recognition where the insane person is recognized, by his society, as a foreigner to his own country; he is not freed from his responsibilities, he is assigned, at least in the form of relationships and of adjoining accomplices, a moral guilt; he is designated as the Other, as the Foreigner, as the Excluded.)

Although the stranger is not directly labelled a *"fou"* and although the bourgeois does not assign any direct moral attributes (except that in the word *"extraordinaire,"* perhaps) the designation *"étranger"* does cast the foreigner into the realm of the Other, of the Incomprehensible, and of the Alien. The system of reasoning and of investigation is not put into question; instead the object of study is cast outside the bourgeois's field of knowledge and outside the margins of his society.

But the text is not quite so simple, because the foreigner is not a passive object of study, nor is he entirely negative and alienating in his replies. While the foreigner's replies preclude further questioning on a specific topic, they are not altogether negative, because they do convey some grains of knowledge, and they do suggest some ambiguous origin. His reply, *"Vous vous servez là d'une parole dont le sens m'est resté jusqu'à ce jour inconnu"* ("You use a word there which to this day has remained unknown to me") implies that *ce jour,* this very day, he learned the meaning of the word *"ami."* Likewise, his declaration *"J'ignore sous quelle latitude elle est située* ("I do not know on what latitude it is situated") leaves open the possibility that he has a country but does not know where it is. There is no physical attachment. Similarly, the use of the conditional *"aimerais"* in *"Je l'aimerais volontiers, déesse et immortelle"* ("I would love it, goddess and immortal") implies that he would love beauty, but there is no way of knowing why he does not. Is it because beauty is a goddess and absolute or because she is not? In the next reply, he turns the tables on the interlocutor when he states *"Je le hais comme vous haïssez Dieu"* ("I hate it as you hate God"). While, for the first time he provides concrete information (I hate gold), he clouds the issue with the astounding information that he seems to know something about the other person (You hate God). How does he know? Previous knowledge? Inferences from the other's questions? A wild guess? A play on the old adage of choosing between money and God? In any case, the foreigner does know where the other person comes from. He knows perfectly the other's context, and in a sense, can nail him without asking any questions. It should be noted that his knowledge is completely negative—what is hated rather than what is loved, and absence, not presence (no God versus a god). The stranger knows the other, he can speak his language, but he does so in order to stop the line of questioning. The result is amazement, not edification.

Out of this dialogue we can make a fairly accurate portrait of the questioner, just as the foreigner seems to be able to infer values.

However, the foreigner is in partial ignorance of the other's society, as he demonstrates by not knowing the meaning of the word "friendship." However, at the same time, he knows more than the other man. In addition, his choice of clouds as his only love places him squarely outside the epistemology and the mores of the bourgeois interlocutor. In a "normal" world, the foreigner would literally be *aliéné*. As a metaphor for the foreigner, the clouds escape definition and stand as "other." They can be seen, but they cannot be seized, nor can they be immobilized into categories, as the bourgeois would want. One can say that they contradict what the questioner stands for and seeks. At the same time, they are a part of his world but they are separate, just as the foreigner stands outside the society while being a part of its world.

One can argue that *"L'Etranger"* brings into a collision course two texts or two textual strategies, where there is no real dialogue. The first strategy is that collection of discourses which the bourgeois relies upon in order to articulate his statements: the importance of the family, friends, country, and so forth. Implicit in the bourgeois's discourse is the notion that language exists to categorize and to immobilize. Also implicit in his discourse is a hierarchy of superior questioner and inferior respondent. The directness of the questions barely hides a belief that language itself is but a transparent tool to aggressively ferret out the truth. The other textual strategy, that of the foreigner, is one of reacting, and his reactions to the questions, refusing any clear affirmations. Instead, he denies or circumvents questions, and uses ambiguous discourse.

The lack of dialogue cannot be dismissed as a mere lack of "communication" or an inability to find a common ground of discourse. Rather, the absurdity of the encounter is derived from diametrically opposed systems of values. The bourgeois knows what he loves and what he values. His priorities are those necessary for the maintenance of a stable society, and his aggressive search for knowledge represents his society's belief that progress can be assured through the pursuit of knowledge. While rejecting all these values, the stranger goes even further. He denies the "here and now," the immediacy of concrete existence, and embraces the marvelous (*merveilleux*—the astonishing or the admirable). The marvelous clouds stand as an inexplicable and supernatural antipode to the values of society. By identifying the clouds as his one love, the stranger not only negates the bourgeois pursuit of knowledge, but he also rejects the materialistic "here and now" implicit in the interlocutor's urgent questions. The stranger loves something which he can never touch and can never possess. While he is alienated from society, he is separated physically from the clouds and attached to them emotionally. Because he adheres to a philosophy of ignorance (he can only "know" the clouds as marvelous things), he thus refuses to grant the knowledge that the bourgeois is seeking, and consequently, knowledge, like a cloud, passes through the text, unattainable and undefinable.

The clouds call into question the very nature of codes and encoding and the very nature of language. Taken literally, they could lead one to conclude that the stranger is in fact a little mad, a true *aliéné*. But they also lend themselves to a broader metaphorical reading of the undefin-able, the unattainable, and the mobile. The text never finalizes the clouds and never gives them precise meaning. Thus, the word cloud floats between language systems and defies precise meaning.

Taken as a whole, the text represents two extremes in discursive practice and in systems of values which can be regarded as the outer limits of the discourses and values found in *Le Spleen de Paris*. In other words, Baudelaire is announcing the thematic strategies, the modes of characterization, the potential languages, and the philosoph-ical breadth of his work. This establishment of parameters is con-firmed in a text which is complementary to *"L'Etranger,"* a short piece entitled *"La Soupe et les nuages."*

In *"La Soupe et les nuages,"* the situation is the opposite. First of all, the narrator is present in his text in the first person. There is also a clear context, that of kitchen in a Parisian apartment, where a woman, not the bourgeois, is preparing the meal and the man turns toward the window to look at the clouds, "the marvelous constructions of the impalpable." Unlike the stranger, who defines the clouds on their own terms, the narrator creates a metaphorical relationship between the clouds and the eyes of his loved one, but it is a rather strange comparison, because he first calls the clouds *"fantasmagories,"* and then states that they are almost as beautiful as the eyes of his mistress, whom he refers to as *"la petite folle monstrueuse aux yeux verts"* ("the monstrous crazy woman with green eyes"). While the clouds and the woman share beauty, they come from different worlds: The clouds recall phantoms and the unreal, while the woman is a crazy monster. Whereas the clouds of *"L'Etranger"* were distant, these are brought to the edge of reality. At the same time, the woman is marked as all too present. If the narrator sought a poetic means to join clouds and woman, one can say that his attempt brought out more differences than similarities. It is not surprising, given the incompatibilities be-tween clouds and woman as seen by the narrator-poet, that no dialogue ensues. Instead, the "poet" is jerked back to reality when the woman violently punches him in the back and says *"Allez-vous bientôt manger votre soupe, s . . . b . . . de marchand de nuages?"* ("Are you going to come and eat your soup, s.o.b. cloud merchant?"). Elusive language gives way to concrete vulgarities.

How, then, do we situate this text in relationship to *"L'Etranger"*?

First, the text revolves around contrasting contexts, the domestic interior and the sky. In *"L'Etranger"* the context—the outside—is only vaguely implied. In addition, unlike the stranger, who never tried to metaphorize the clouds, the narrator contemplates and seeks to render them poetic. But in the comparison, the clouds lose their absolute value, because they are *used* as a means to define the beauty of the woman's eyes. In other words, the clouds become a part of the narrator-poet's world. Of greatest importance, *"La Soupe et les nuages"* lays bare what is implicit in the first text. *"L'Etranger"* functioned in part as a failed economy of discourse, where the bourgeois sought to possess the other's knowledge and where he expected an exchange. But the possession and exchange were constantly denied. The stranger apparently owned nothing and gave almost nothing. In the present text, there remains a conflict of discourses, but they are now on two different levels. On one hand, the "poet" turns his back on his mistress to create in his mind a poetic statement. In exchange, he is attacked physically and accused of being a cloud merchant. His poetic efforts are reduced to the most crass economic level, and the clouds lose the purity they had in the first text. They are now just like everything else in society. Within a very precise context of his society, that of the apartment, the poet, as poet, and his discourse are metaphorically killed: The woman has decoded and domesticated him before placing him in front of his soup bowl. She recalls the bourgeois of *"L'Etranger"* because she also is firmly anchored in the material world. However, she, unlike the bourgeois, has all the answers and knows how to act on them. Further, she, not the poet, has the final world. Whereas the stranger retained power over the bourgeois by his enigmatic final statement, the poet is literally beaten at his own game. At the same time, the clouds are also killed and reborn as objects of exchange.

It would be contradictory to say that the stranger represents an ideal state of alienation. However, his discourse, or lack of it, and his love of the distant clouds do suggest that he is in a pure state, untouched and unharmed by society. His counterpart represents the imposition of the real world and the mercantile exchange system, the triumph of decoding and metaphorical death.

Where is *the* poet in all this? One might be tempted to identify the stranger as the ideal poet, yet there is nothing in the text to suggest such a decoding because the stranger never comes close to using poetic language. To the contrary, his description of the clouds represents an empty signifier which he never fills with meaning. At the same time Baudelaire, the third person narrator, never enters into the text. He simulates the role of a scribe, recording the words of others. Conversely, the poet of *"La Soupe et les nuages"* can be seen as the poet in modern society. The use of the first person pronoun could lead one to identify him as Baudelaire himself. But, as suggested earlier, he is not a terribly good poet. By joining the texts together (joining fragmented ends of the snake), we have one poet who is invisible and another who is too visible, with his soupy clouds. Whereas the poet stays out of the context in *"L'Etranger,"* he is highly encoded in the second text. He is both in the text and out of it, personal and impersonal.

This very search for the poet implies the existence of a reader, who has been present throughout this study. My purpose here has been to explain, to clarify, and to locate the contexts of two short texts by Baudelaire. Yet, my ultimate aim has been to decode Baudelaire. In Bakhtin's terms, I have sought to kill context. But the discussion of the position of the poet in/out of the text suggests that the attempts to decode them are illusory: If interpretations have been brought forward, they are at their most tentative because the decoding took both texts out of their context in *Le Spleen de Paris.* Yet Baudelaire, in his preface stated that the prose poems could—and should—be taken out of order to create new contexts. In other words, the two prose poems are free to float, like clouds, among other prose poems, where new limited contexts can be created and where new forms of decoding can be reenacted. There is no question that Baudelaire provides the reader with fairly precise codes, but, because the context can constantly change, the death that decoding implies is merely a temporary one. The texts succeed in escaping death as they alternate between shifting codes and elusive contexts. You cannot kill a cloud.

Notes

1. M. M. Bakhtin, *Speech Genres and Other Late Essays* (Austin: University of Texas Press, 1986), 147.

2. Suzanne Bernard, *Le Poème en prose de Baudelaire jusqu'à nos jours* (Paris: Nizet, 1959); Barbara Johnson, *Défigurations du langage poétique* (Paris: Flammarion, 1979). The translation from Baudelaire's poem below is my own.

3. For more detailed discussion of the question, see Theodore Zeldin, *France 1848–1945* (Oxford: The Clarendon Press, 1977) and Richard Terdiman *Discourse/Counter-Discourse* (Ithaca: Cornell University Press, 1985).

4. Special thanks are due to Professor Gwenhaël Bonnau, Departmental Chair at the Université de Nantes, who suggested this idea during discussion at the conference.

5. Michel Foucault, *Histoire de la folie à l'âge classique* (Paris, Gallimard: 1972), 148.

The Nocturne in *fin-de-siècle* Paris

WILLIAM SHARPE

One of the most intriguing ways in which poets and painters of the *fin de siècle* looked forward artistically—by looking back to earlier traditions—was in their representation of night. In 1893, William Sharp, a British Decadent poet, and friend of Yeats and Symons, published a free-verse poem entitled "A Paris Nocturne." The title and subject matter—the Seine as it flows through nighttime Paris—recalled Verlaine's "*Nocturne parisien*" and Corbière's "*Paris Nocturne*," as well as evoking a host of poems simply labeled "Nocturne" by Jean Moréas, Jules Laforgue, Gustave Kahn, and others. In the same year, the elegantly eccentric Count Robert de Montesquiou-Ferensac, model for Huysmans' des Esseintes, included in his collection *Les Chauves-Souris (The Bats)* a group of poems named "Penumbras (Twice Thirteen Nocturnes)." Dedicated to Whistler, Montesquiou-Ferensac's book acknowledged a British visual influence as much as Sharp's poem alluded to its French literary genealogy.

Seemingly insignificant, this crossing of lines of influence among minor figures of the *fin de siècle* indicates in fact an important strand in the fabrication of Modernism. For there was, during the later nineteenth century, a widespread fascination with night and the nocturne as a progressive artistic form. The prose poems of Baudelaire's *Le Spleen de Paris* were first entitled *Poèmes nocturnes;* Redon's *Nocturne* and his etchings of night owe much to the Symbolist poets; Rimbaud was sufficiently aware of the form to wish to challenge it in his "*Nocturne vulgaire*." Related to the "*clair de lune*" or "moonlight" topos popular in both poetry and painting for more than a century, the nocturne emerged after 1860 as a lyric mode of expression allowing highly subjective meditations on the states of perception intensified by darkness.

Retrospectively, we can see that the very imprecision of the form was part of its attraction, as the nocturne became one of the foremost expressions of the movement toward synesthesia. For during this period the autonomy of the individual arts was being assaulted through a variety of new combinations. In 1852, Théophile Gautier published his poem *"Symphonie en blanc majeur"* ("Symphony in White Major"); in 1854, Franz Liszt coined the musical term "symphonic poem"; in 1867, Whistler first gave a musical title to one of his canvases, the *Symphony in White, no. 3;* and when Debussy applied the title "Nocturnes" to one of his symphonic poems a few decades later, he was thinking of neither music nor literature but of Whistler's art. Poets and painters seeking to explore the shadowy areas between the abstract, aural, temporal nature of music, and the representational, visual, spatial nature of art discovered that they could readily enter this aesthetic frontier by taking darkness itself as their subject. Thus, after about 1875, those who called their works "Nocturnes" could imagine themselves participating in a literary, musical, or artistic tradition, and perhaps all three. The fluidity of the term suggests the fluidity of artistic boundaries that most of these poets and artists strove to reexamine.

I

The title "nocturne" was originally given in the 1820s by Field, Chopin, and others to a type of dreamy musical composition. But within a few decades, poets and painters began to apply the word to atmospheric night scenes, often of rivers flowing through the midst of darkened cities. One can trace a tradition of French urban night painting from Robert DeMachy's fireworks and fires in the later eighteenth century, such as *The Foire St. Germain on Fire* (1763) and *Fireworks on the Place Louis XV* (1782) to Johan Barthold Jongkind's numerous moonlight views of the Seine in the 1850s, such as *Clair de lune sur la Seine* (1855). But the idea of the nocturne as an evocative, atmospheric artistic form had the greatest impact in England, thanks to the work of Whistler, and it was largely through Whistler's influence that the harmonious and nuanced portrayals of nocturnal urban beauty achieved popularity in France toward the end of the century.[1]

Having studied in Paris in the 1850s, Whistler imported the aesthetic of *l'art pour l'art* or "art for art's sake" to London when he moved there in 1859, along with a belief in the interpenetration of poetry, painting, and music. His nocturnal views of the Thames became the subject of public controversy in the 1870s, and his spirited defense of them against Ruskin in 1878 marked a turning point in English art and taste. Under the spell of Whistler and the French writers from Gautier to Mallarmé, whom he championed, English poets including Wilde, Symons, Henley, and Douglas made the

London nocturne one of the most characteristic expressions of the Aesthetic Movement of the 1880s and 1890s. Moody, evocative, aspiring to a musical freedom from denotation even as it claimed mimetic accuracy, in England the nocturne undermined the intense particularity and self-consciousness of high Victorian poetry and painting, becoming a bridge to Imagism and abstraction.

Whistler began painting nocturnes in 1866, but not until 1872, when he produced the *Nocturne in Blue and Gold: Old Battersea Bridge* (1872-75), did he begin to use the title "Nocturne," making the term notorious in London.[2] Whistler expressed his aesthetic theory provocatively in his famous "Ten O'Clock Lecture" of 1885:

> When the evening mist clothes the riverside with poetry, as with a veil, and the poor buildings lose themselves in the dim sky, and the tall chimneys become campanili, and the warehouses are palaces in the night, and the whole city hangs in the heavens, and fairy-land is before us—then . . . Nature, who, for once, has sung in tune, sings her exquisite song to the artist alone.[3]

As night transforms the city, so the nocturne altered expectations about the sorts of truths art should reveal, subversively posing its delicate balance of romantic mystery and abstract form against the mainstream preoccupation with narrative and hard-edged mimeticism. Works such as the *Nocturne in Blue and Gold: Old Battersea Bridge* taught viewers to see the urban landscape in a new way, enhancing it with rain and mist, but not disguising its bold, distinctive architectural forms.

One reason why Whistler's vision could be so quickly assimilated was the fact that a strong tradition of painting the river Thames, often at night, already existed. Major artists of the Romantic and Victorian eras such as J. M. W. Turner (*Moonlight: A Study at Millbank* [1797]) and William Holman Hunt (*View from a Window in Cheyne Walk* [1853]) repeatedly sought to capture the effect of moonlight on the river; other artists whose nighttime Thames views preceded those of Whistler include G. P. Boyce and a whole family devoted to moonlights—William, Sebastian, and Henry Pether. In the wake of Whistler, artists such as Atkinson Grimshaw, Walter Greaves, and T. R. Way also worked in the same vein. The vast majority of London night views are of the Thames, and almost all of them convey a subtle, quiet, pensive mood.

Similarly, the English poets of the 1880s and 1890s such as Oscar Wilde, William Ernest Henley, Alfred Douglas, and Arthur Symons were attracted to the Whistlerian vision of the darkened city, and though their subjects were more varied than those of the painters, they

Whistler. *Old Battersea Bridge.* 1872–75. Courtesy of Tate Gallery Publications, London.

all sought to convey the beauties of dark masses and scattered lights, reflective water and silent streets. Wilde acknowledged Whistler's influence in *"Impression du Matin"* (1880); Henley paid him homage in "To James McNeil Whistler" (1889); and in the 1890s, in poems such as "Nocturne," "April Midnight," "The Abandoned," and others, Symons devoted more attention than anyone to nocturnal city scenes.

II

In France, the situation was far less unified aesthetically than in Britain. Of course, in both countries there were allegorical or symbolic representations of night, based on gauze-wrapped female figures. Examples include *Night* (1897) by Whistler's friend from his student days, Henri Fantin-Latour, and *Summer Night* (ca. 1890) by one of Whistler's closest English associates, Albert Moore. And there is also a European tradition of nocturnal marine subjects that influenced not only Turner's *Fishermen at Sea* (1798), the first major canvas he showed at the Royal Academy, but also Manet's *Moonlight on Boulogne Harbor* (1869) and Monet's *Marine* (ca. 1866).

But the effort made by painters from 1870 to 1900 to represent Paris at night results in something quite different from the Whistlerian aesthetic dominant in England at the same time. Paul Verlaine's oft-cited dictum, in *"Art poétique,"* that only the "nuance" should matter seems initially to have been more influential among painters abroad than in France. For Parisian artists such as Degas, Seurat, and Pissarro were already captivated by the flare of gas and the glare of reflected artificial light. Unlike London artists who concentrated on dreamy nocturnal river views, these French painters sought to capture the brightly lit social activity of Haussmann's redeveloped Paris.

Consider, for example, Degas' *Femmes devant un café le soir (Women on a Café Terrace, Evening)* (1877). Here night has another meaning—sexual adventure. The women are generally agreed to be prostitutes, and it has been suggested that the woman getting up to leave the café on the left is following a signal given to her by the male figure vanishing on the right.[4] Both of them have their bodies lopped off or concealed by the pillars of the café, as if to indicate that their transaction does not involve the whole person, but only a hastily glimpsed part. The scene is lit by lamps both inside and outside the café, and the glass in the front window reveals and reflects them both. The reflected lights imply that this is a world of deceptive surfaces, where gaslight dispels darkness but does not illuminate the private motives that animate the figures in this public space.

Degas. *Femmes devant un café le soir.* 1877. Courtesy of the Musée d'Orsay, Paris.

Degas. *La Chanson du chien*. Ca. 1875–78. Private collection.

With Degas's *Au Café-concert: la chanson du chien (At the Cabaret: The Song of the Dog)* (1876–78), we move from the Boulevard Montmartre to the park along the Champs-Elysées near the Place de la Concorde. In his views of outdoor cafés concerts, like this one at the Alcazar, Degas conveys a more pronounced sense of the urban night as a theatrical spectacle, fraught with illusion. The singer Thérésa (Emma Valadon) is caught up in her song, imitating a dog, while before her the crowd stirs restlessly. Above them in the trees are the globes of gas lamps, which are also reflected in the mirror behind the singer. The surfaces of singer, mirror, and painting all project a story of refined animality—"She opens her huge mouth," Degas wrote, "and out comes the grossest, the most delicate, the most wittily tender voice there is."[5] The pillar that separates mirror from reality disappears directly into the center of the woman's body, pinning her between the artificially lit stage and the dark park, between song and action, art and desire.

Produced ten years later, Seurat's *Parade de cirque* (1887–88) records another actual nocturnal event, the performances of the Circus Corvi at the Place de la Nation in 1887.[6] But here reality is still further undercut by the stylization of the figures and gas jets, by the peculiar colors, and especially by the flattening of space into a series of abutting rather than receding planes. Contemporary photographs and drawings of the Circus Corvi have helped scholars decipher the intricate visual puzzle—a combination of balustrade, legs, and shadows of legs creates the impression that the musicians on the left have too many feet, while the green rectangle to the right of the central trombone player turns out to be an interior door—the plane in the picture that is actually furthest removed from the spectator.

While Seurat may have done some night sketches, this is a studio picture, closer to the process of traditional painting than to the *plein air* technique of the Impressionists. We know that Seurat was reading works of color theory that included tables showing the alteration of natural colors under gaslight; and in this canvas he may have been trying to apply the recently published theories of Charles Henry, which assigned specific emotional values to lines, forms, and colors. Yet the painting's general theme is not arcane. The friezelike isolation of the figures, the sombre tone of this amusement, the lack of depth where one would expect it—all this indicates the vanity of human pleasures, the superficiality and sadness of entertainments as transitory as life itself. For these reasons, Seurat's painting seems to possess a uniformly melancholy tone that allies it with the canvases of Whistler, whom Seurat admired[7]—a unity of effect that sets the *Parade* apart from the glittering cafés depicted by Degas.

Seurat. *Parade de cirque.* 1887–88. Courtesy of the Metropolitan Museum of Art, New York.

One may sense a similar fascination with the seductive allure of the city at night in Pissarro's *Paris, the Boulevard Montmartre at Night* (ca. 1897), where there is also a Whistlerian touch in its distant, atmospheric view of the city. With the shimmering reflections on the wet pavement, Pissarro turns the rainy street into a river, but it has none of the natural repose of the Thames. The artist's fluid brushwork threatens to dissolve the whole social spectacle. Water—a central element in French poetic nocturnes—seems to drip here from every brush stroke, while the lights of streetlamps, shops, and cabs persevere only to be swallowed by the gulf toward which the perspective pulls our eyes. The nearest and brightest streetlamp stares back at the viewer, a counter-eye with a dark halo that repeats the entire scene in microcosm. There is no specific reason to read the painting as one more comment on the insubstantiality of the Parisian mirror world, but in the context of Degas and Seurat it is difficult not to. The vitality of Pissarro's surface cannot overcome the dominant impression, conveyed by the relentless perspective and the dark sky above, that the ephemeral city is in the process of consuming itself. The words of my namesake, William Sharp, in "A Paris Nocturne" seem apropos:

> And, over all, one light
> Palpitant, circular, wide,
> Sweeping the city vast—
> Yonder, beyond where in shadow
> The thronged Champs-Elysées are filling
> With echoes of human voices,
> With shadows of human lives,
> With phantoms of vampyre-vices. . . .[8]

Although one might sense that the agitated, fragmented city of the Impressionists was ultimately a Chimera, no more substantial than a plate-glass reflection or a thin layer of paint, not until about 1900 did the Whistlerian version of this vulnerability emerge in French painting, in the work of Eugène Carrière and Henri Le Sidaner. Both Carrière's *Place Clichy at Night* (1899–1900) and Le Sidaner's *Moonlight on St. Paul's* (ca. 1901) have much in common with Whistler's nocturnal street scenes, such as *Nocturne: Trafalgar Square, Chelsea—Snow* (1875–77). All three artists use darkness and dense atmospheric effects to blur the city into a few delicately toned, nearly abstract forms that suggest far more than they say. The influence of Whistler is also felt directly by this time through the agency of Whistler's "Ten O'Clock" lecture—which Mallarmé had translated into French in 1888—and indirectly through Debussy's "Nocturnes," which were first performed in 1900. Having been shaped by the Parisian artistic

Figure. Boulevard Montmartre at Night, Ca. 1897. Courtesy of the National Gallery London.

milieu in the 1850s, Whistler's ideas did not seem foreign to the Symbolists. Indeed, they appeared very much in the ascendency by 1905 when the critic Camille Mauclair proclaimed that the inevitable fusion of the arts would prove that their deepest principles were identical; that the arts of Debussy, Whistler, and Le Sidaner were all analogous; and that the nocturnes of Whistler and Le Sidaner were rising out of the ruins of tradition to furnish "the aesthetic of the future."[9]

III

Just as the French painters were creating a new art of the city after dark, poets were using the nocturne to explore both city and psyche. But in France there appears to be a split between night poems specifically about Paris and those labeled simply "nocturne" that feature a delocalized landscape of human emotion. The urban group includes poems such as Verlaine's *"Nocturne parisien"* (1866); Corbière's *"Paris nocturne"* (1873; pub. 1890); and Laforgue's *"Litanies nocturnes"* (1880). In their use of the nighttime city to reflect the fevered state of urban consciousness, these poems could be said to descend from Baudelaire's *Tableaux parisiens* and *Spleen de Paris*. But whereas Baudelaire rapturously proclaims in the prose poem *"Crépuscule du soir"*: *"O nuit! . . . vous êtes le feu d'artifice de la déesse Liberté!"* ("O night! . . . you are the fireworks of the goddess Liberty!"), his successors use night to reveal and even mock the desperation of the human condition.

In Verlaine's *"Nocturne parisien"* (1866), one can identify some of the poetic nocturne's main characteristics, such as the omnipresence of water imagery, the preoccupation with death and corpses, dreams and music, the sense of the city's enormity and implacability. With the sounds of an organ grinder at sunset, Verlaine's Paris melts into a synesthetic harmony of light and color, music, and plastic form. But after dark, as the gaslights come on, the stars and lights reflected in the silent black river recall the murderous aspect of the Seine established in the first stanza, and the river's paradoxical power to make its deadliness the source of artistic creativity:

> *Roule, roule, ton flot indolent, morne Seine,*
> *Sous tes ponts qu'environne une vapeur malsaine*
> *Bien des corps ont passé, morts, horribles, pourris,*
> *Dont les âmes avaient pour meurtrier Paris.*

Mais tu n'en traînes pas, en tes ondes glacées,
Autant que ton aspect m'inspire de pensées!

(Roll, gloomy Seine, roll down your indolent flood, / under your bridges where sickly vapors brood / how many a body's passed, dead, bloated, foul, / and it is Paris that has killed the soul. / But nothing drifts along your icy stream / so powerful as your face to make me dream!)[10]

"Paris, l'Onde et la Nuit" ("Paris, the Deep, and Night"), which the poet addresses as a *"Sinistre trinité,"* emerge as three unholy versions of death which the serpentine Seine *("vieux serpent")* will inexorably bring to urban mortals. Here there is a Fall but no redemption. Because the snakelike river will "flow forever," it becomes for Verlaine an eternal image of time, a river of hell, that makes the Parisian night a permanent condition. This Stygian stream perversely carries but cannot ignite the fuel—coal, lumber, cadavers—that it distributes. Instead, this cargo fires the poet's imagination; however many corpses the river bears, he says, it cannot equal the number of dark thoughts that the mere sight of the Seine inspires in him: *"Tu n'en traînes pas, en tes ondes glacées, / autant que ton aspect m'inspire de pensées!"* For Verlaine, night is the means of laying bare the psychological torments of the city, and the suicides and victims who float in the river give both literal and metaphoric evidence that Paris is a murderer who ironically helps keep the poet's art alive.

Corbière's "Paris Nocturne" (ca. 1873) is more schematic and more distanced from contemporary urban observation than Verlaine's death-ridden meditation on the Seine. The city is not directly described but insistently metaphorized, as the sea, the river Styx, a field, death, and finally life itself. In keeping with the epigraph—*"Ce n'est pas une ville, c'est un monde,"* ("It's not a city; it's a world")—each stanza seems to contain its opposite.[11] The calm sea gives way to the roar of the waves; the Styx is dried up, but poets fish in it, and so on to the last stanza where city life is equated with living death:

C'est la vie: Ecoutez: la source vive chante
L'éternelle chanson sur la tête gluante
D'un dieu marin tirant ses membres nus et verts
Sur le lit de la morgue . . . Et les yeux grand ouverts!

(It is life: Listen: the live stream is singing / The eternal song on the slimy head / Of a sea-god stretching his limbs naked and green / On a bed of the Morgue . . . With his eyes wide open!)

Even more explicitly than in Verlaine's poem, such morbidly musical rivers, streams, and fountains perversely refresh the parched brain of the poet; from them he fishes for inspiration: *"Le long du ruisseau noir, les poètes pervers / Pêchent: leur crâne creux leur sert de boîte à vers"* ("All along the black stream, depraved poets / Fish; from empty skulls they bait their lines"). But the price of hooking this *chanson éternelle* is that one cannot then cut it loose. In a nightmarish world-city where the darker side of greco-roman mythology (Diogenes, harpies, river-gods, the Styx) mingles with the worst of the present—thieves, police, the morgue—the exposure to such sights bestows upon the poet (and hence the reader, too) the torment of the insomniac and the zombie: the fate of having to keep one's anguished eyes wide open. The orderliness of Corbière's couplets barely contains the terrors he sees in the night, and the many sounds that he describes compete with the silence of death: *"Ecoutez: pas un rêve ne bouge"* ("Listen . . . not a dream is moving").

Jules Laforgue's *"Litanies nocturnes"* (1880) assaults from a different angle the peace that one expects to prevail in a nocturne, by parodying the ecclesiastical origins of the nocturne form. A nocturne is one of the offices sung in the night in a monastery, and a litany is a prayer of supplication. But in Laforgue's poem, God is cursed, not entreated:

> *Sur la Terre, là-bas, en France*
> *Et sur ce point nommé Paris*
> *Un gueux n'a pas même un radis*
> *Pour se lester un peu la panse.*
>
> *Pas un radis. En conséquence*
> *Il crève au fond de son taudis,*
> *En criant: Dieu, je te maudis!*
> *C'est la nuit calme et le silence.*

(On earth, yonder, in France and in that place named Paris, a beggar has not even a sou to help fill his belly. Not a sou. And so he dies at the back of his hovel, crying out, 'God, I curse you!' The night is calm and silent.)

Like Corbière, Laforgue transmutes the visual play of light and shadow found in night painting into a poetic, aural tension that sets nocturnal silence against urban noise.[12] The strategy of the poem is to imply a dark, despair-inducing soundlessness through the medium of verbal music, and yet Laforgue undercuts it with his intimate, familiar language. The last line just quoted, *"C'est la nuit calme et le silence,"* thus creates a double tension. Repeated at, or near, the end of each of the poem's nine sections, it quietly conveys the deafness of God to human pleas. But it also can seem rather pompous in the presence of colloquialisms like *"panse"* and *"radis,"* thereby making the whole situation even more pitiful, more a matter of human anxieties than divine abandonment. Where Corbière's reiterated *"C'est"* is aggressive, definitive, Laforgue's use of the construction denies that there is any new information—the night continues, oblivious to the cries of doubt-racked Parisians. As the poet concludes,

> *On te blasphème et l'on t'encense*
> *Et jamais tu ne répondis,*
> *Les mortels en sont ébahis.*
> *Ce qui t'absout c'est ton absence.*

("We blaspheme against you and we send you incense, and you never answer; we mortals are staggered by it. What absolves you is your absence.")

In a series of ironic reversals, direct address produces no response, speech guarantees silence, the divine Light and Presence remains occluded and absent, and God needs absolution. For Laforgue, nighttime gives voice to life's most unanswerable questions, encouraging the poet to cry out and mock his despair at the same time, to turn complaint into creation by self-consciously breaking the silence he invokes.[13]

There is space to mention only briefly the group of poems and prose-poems called "Nocturne" that, between 1860 and 1900, rejected the urban world and departed even from such unseen landscapes as Laforgue's. Among the authors of a "Nocturne" are Albert Glatigny (1864), Charles Cros (1869), Paul Bourget (1872), Laforgue (1880), Gustave Kahn (1886), Jean Moréas (1895), and Albert Samain (ca. 1893). There were also other, more elaborate nocturnes, such as those of Montesquiou-Ferensac, designed to capture the entire cycle of nighttime emotions, *"une concentration du mystère nocturne."*[14] These delocalized, self-consciously musical poems appear to stem initially from Chopin, although by the 1880s Whistler had become influential. There is rarely a specifiable subject, only an often melancholic mood without a location, replete with images of waves, flowers, perfumes, and colors.[15]

Products of a synesthetic sensibility that finds harmony and color in words as well as in sounds and images, such poems are related to the *"clair de lune"* tradition that in painting includes Vernet, Millet, and Jongkind, and in poetry includes poems by Leconte de Lisle (1861) and Verlaine (1867). The *"clair de lune"* usually shines on a rural landscape, but as Verlaine's poem reveals, the poet's objective is to use the transformative effect of moonlight to gain access to hidden emotions. Thus his "Clair de lune" begins, *"Votre âme est un paysage choisi"* ("Your soul is a carefully chosen landscape"); the poet's vision becomes interiorized, the landscape psychological. Rimbaud's "Nocturne vulgaire" (ca. 1877) pushes this process further, and in a sense sets the tone for subsequent journeys into the darkness, by focusing on the dissolution of physical and mental boundaries. With the last line he erases all the familiar limits of home and daytime: *"Un souffle disperse les limites du foyer"* ("A breath disperses the boundaries of the hearth"). Finally, Gustave Kahn's "Nocturne" (1886), like Montesquiou-Ferensac's series, is clearly inspired by Whistler, both poets abandoning landscape altogether for synesthetic evocations of evanescent color, shadow, and sound: *"Un peu de blond, un peu de bleu, un peu de blanc . . . / Un peu de son, des parfums doux et du très lent"* ("A little blond, a little blue, a little white . . . a little sound, some sweet perfumes, and [play it] very slowly").

IV

Historically, artists and critics have viewed the shifting relations between the arts in different periods as a constant struggle for hegemony.[16] From this perspective, the emergence of the nocturne might be read as a validation of Walter Pater's late-Victorian theory that "all art constantly aspires towards the condition of music." To embrace the elusive, non-denotative qualities of night would be thus to challenge literary or artistic conventions valuing daylight, rationality, and the customary activities of daily social life. And so by about 1900, both poetry and painting reach into more private realms, and symbolism and Whistlerian tonality come to the fore. As Kahn explains about the Symbolists, *"Le but essentiel de notre art est d'objectiver le subjectif (l'extériorisation de l'Idée) au lieu de subjectiver l'objectif (la nature vue à travers un tempérament)"* ("The essential aim of our art is to objectify the subjective [the exteriorization of the Idea] rather than subjectify the objective [nature seen through the lens of a single temperament])."[17] Such a theory, he claims, has affected all the arts, producing the multi-tonal work of Wagner as well as the new techniques of the Neo-Impressionists. This, I believe, is part of the story, but not all of it. For the nocturne is a liminal form *par excellence*. While it questions many boundaries, it fully transgresses few, tranquilly yet troublingly occupying the contested ground between public and private realms, mimesis and abstraction, romanticism and modernism, waking and dreaming.

In probing these shadows, the French do not seem to give special emphasis to the idea that the city itself is lovely at night. It may be that after a century of industrialization, the English, through Whistler's eyes, were rediscovering a sense of urban beauty, while Parisians had never lost it. Through their stylistic innovations, they pursued the meaning of their unflagging attraction to Paris into unlikely places, and subjected the sources of inspiration to the often harsh glare of their cultural and moral analysis. Poets like Corbière, Verlaine, and Laforgue stretched the nocturnal genre by pitting the agitated emotions and sinister aspects of the city—desperate loneliness, crime, horror, morbidity, mortality—against the conventions of late-night stillness and peace. Meanwhile, Degas, Seurat, and Pissarro preferred artificially illuminated public activities to traditional scenes of tranquil moonlight, even as such landscapes were being revolutionized by Whistler. In *fin-de-siècle* Paris, poets and painters were balancing public and private, mimetic and formal concerns, as they used the gaslit metropolis to explore social surfaces and their own emotional depths. The close attention that such diverse talents gave to nocturnal representation at this time suggests that, even though they all dealt with a specifically Parisian night, their shared interest in nocturnal subjects was only a starting point from which each, in his own way, might pursue a new aesthetic to illuminate the heart of a modernist darkness.

Notes

1. The nocturne can thus be considered a flexible category within the larger designation "representation of night." The chief characteristic of the nocturne is its dreamy, reflective, atmospheric quality, and I am concerned here with how poets and painters conveyed (while occasionally undercutting) this mood when they portrayed a subject that might at first seem antithetical to nocturnal repose—the modern urban landscape.

2. The word "nocturne" is defined by the *OED* as a musical, artistic, or literary work having a "dreamy character" appropriate to nighttime. But the first instance the *OED* cites of the term being applied to painting is this anti-Whistlerian warning to artists: "don't be bothered with symphonies and nocturnes" (1874; R. Turwhitt, *Sketch Club* 300).

3. "Mr. Whistler's Ten O'Clock," *The Gentle Art of Making Enemies* (London: Heineman, 1892), 144.

4. See Robert L. Herbert, *Impressionism: Art, Leisure, and Parisian Society* (New Haven: Yale University Press, 1988), 44–45.

5. Letter to Henri Lerolle, 4 Dec. 1883, in *Lettres de Degas*, ed. Marcel Guérin (Paris, 1945), 75; cited in Herbert, 83.

6. For an extensive analysis of the painting in relation both to Parisian sideshows and to Neo-Impressionist aesthetics, see Robert L. Herbert, *"Parade de cirque* de Seurat et l'esthétique scientifique de Charles Henry," *Revue de l'art* 50 (1980): 9–23, and Robert L. Herbert et al., *Georges Seurat 1859–1891* (New York: Metropolitan

Museum of Art, 1991), 305–311, 391–93. I am indebted to Herbert for many of the points I make here.

7. See Gustave Kahn, *"Chronique: Les Peintres étrangers à l'Exposition," La Vogue* (1889): 223.

8. *The Symbolist Poem: The Development of the English Tradition,* ed. Edward Engelberg (New York: Dutton, 1967), 216–17. Cf. also the excited evening activity of Laforgue's "Soir de Carnaval" (ca. 1880): *"Paris chahute au gaz. L'horloge comme un glas / Sonne une heure. Chantez! dansez! / . . . la vie est brève, / Tout est vain"* ("Paris kicks up its heels in the gaslight. The clock like a knell sounds one A.M.: sing! dance! . . . Life is short, all is in vain"). Unless otherwise noted, translations used in this essay are my own.

9. Camille Mauclair, *De Watteau à Whistler* (Paris: Charpentier, 1905), 245–50.

10. Paul Verlaine, *Selected Poems,* trans. C. F. MacIntyre (Berkeley: University of California Press, 1970), 41.

11. Quotations from this poem translated by Kenneth Koch and Georges Guy, *An Anthology of French Poetry from Nerval to Valéry,* ed. Angel Flores (Garden City, N.Y.: Doubleday, 1958), 80.

12. Perhaps the most striking example of this technique is Baudelaire's "Les Aveugles," where the poet defines the *"noir illimité"* ("boundless darkness") of the blind men as *"ce frère du silence éternel"* ("that brother of eternal silence"), a silence he then contrasts to the city that bellows around them. See William Sharpe, *Unreal Cities: Urban Figuration in Wordsworth, Baudelaire, Whitman, Eliot, and Williams* (Baltimore: Johns Hopkins University Press, 1990), 53–56.

13. See also Laforgue's "Soir de Carnaval" (c. 1880): *"Aux fêtes d'ici-bas, j'ai toujours sangloté: / 'Vanité, vanité, tout n'est que vanité!' / —Puis je songeais: où sont les cendres du Psalmiste?"* ("At the celebrations here below I have always sobbed, 'Vanity, vanity, all is vanity,' —but then I wonder: where are the ashes of the Psalmist?") I would here like to thank Michele Hannoosh, of the University of California at Davis, for her suggestions regarding Laforgue and the representation of Paris in general.

14. Comte Robert de Montesquiou-Ferensac, *Les Chauves-souris* (Paris: Ricard, 1893), V. Henri Lavedan also produced a collection of sixteen dramatic sketches taking place in Paris at night that he called *Nocturnes* (1891); he sent an inscribed copy to Whistler.

15. There is no room here to detail the complex history of moonlight as a motif in nineteenth-century French poetry, but it should be noted that Laforgue, for one, consistently parodies the romantic preoccupation of lovers with the moon in such works as his *L'Imitation de Notre-Dame la Lune* (1885) and *"Spleen des nuits de juillet."* Meanwhile Verlaine in his *"Effet de nuit"* ("Night Effect") (1866) and his *"Croquis parisien"* ("Parisian Sketch") (1866) ignores conventional themes to focus on the grim or mundane features of the city at night.

16. See W. J. T. Mitchell, *Iconology: Image, Text, Ideology* (Chicago: University of Chicago Press, 1986), 94–113.

17. Cited by Octave Malivert (pseudonym), *"La genèse du symbolisme," La Vie moderne* 8, 20 Nov. 1886, 742.

PART 3
History and Its Texts

Revolutionary Signs and Discourse

JEAN-JACQUES THOMAS

Hugo, Vallès, Zola

Nineteen eighty-nine is the year of the bicentennial of the French Revolution, but, given the numerous historical references with which the French patrimony is encumbered, every year could be the occasion to celebrate a person or an institution. A celebration is, however, never neutral. Today, for example, which Revolution are we celebrating? The Revolution represented by the storming of the Bastille? The Terror? The Tenth of Thermidor? The *Declaration of the Rights of Man?* To each his own revolutionary image, and we need François Furet's patience and courage to recall that the Revolution is not one vast, homogenous field of study. The same goes for literature. The writers who might be chosen to emblematize one image or another of our "revolutionary" past are innumerable.

Thus, recently, in France, we celebrated the centennial of the death of Victor Hugo, but at the same time, we chose to ignore the centennial of Jules Vallès. They both died during the same year, and both, in one guise or another, embodied a certain idea of revolutionary writing. Thus, nothing could be more noteworthy than the difference in the treatment that posterity has reserved for these two victims of 1885.

On the one hand, France raised its voice in unison to celebrate Hugo; from orthodox Marxists to the conservative members of the *"Club de l'Horloge,"* they honored pell-mell the visionary, the democrat, the social thinker, the republican, the writer, the genius, the revolutionary populist. This ideological jumble was astutely staged by the socialist regime, and its rare detractors were given a severe thrashing in an editorial from the liberal newspaper *Le Monde*. Not a single note was sounded off-key for this veritable "family affair." In the

---

Translations by Juliette Rogers.

name of national culture, the entire French community encircled the remains of the great popular voice which incarnates the revolutionary ideals of 1789. It was a matter of xenophobia turned inside out—a kind of "Hands off my Hugo!"—as was clearly proved in the commemorative issue of *Europe*, to which not a single foreign intellectual, scholar, or researcher was invited to contribute.

Nothing like this marks the centennial of Jules Vallès. One searches in vain for a glorious celebration, official or otherwise. One century after his disappearance, his situation has not changed: He remains excluded from the gold medalists of great literature. His inability to achieve the renown which is his due reveals a double failure: the failure of his work and the failure of the generation of "forty-eighters" of whom he is the most active representative. For, as Philippe Bonnefis reminds us in his facetious work *Vallès: Du bon usage de la lame et de l'aiguille (Vallès: the Correct Use of the Blade and the Needle)*,[1] Vallès's central project consisted in producing a novel where "will be told the misfortunes of his generation."

"Generation" is a theme dear to socialist France in 1989, and if, today, it is the *"Mitterrand Generation"* which is celebrating the bicentennial of the Revolution, we must not confuse *post-revolutionary banquets* with *soup kitchens* . . .

However, it was in this function of *populist eulogy* that Vallès's Jacques Vingtras trilogy (*L'Enfant, Le Bachelier, l'Insurgé*) was meant to play. These novels tell the story of disinherited youths who were twenty in 1848 and who could only briefly fulfill their dreams during the dark days of the Paris Commune in 1870. An entire generation lost, forgotten, or unloved, appearing only in the novels of this well-off and well-established elders' cliché of displaced and out-of-date intellectual mediocrity: *la Bohême*. The typical image is that of a young man of modest and provincial origins who arrives in Paris manifestly influenced by an incomplete and informal education; he is a prisoner of chronic financial difficulties which force him to make a living from temporary, freelance writing assignments in marginal journals and to hang out in cafés with other young people who are all as poor and as imprisoned as he. This stereotypical portrait, in general, corresponds to Vallès's biography, even if the latter goes a bit beyond the ordinary in his role as editor of the popular newspapers *La Rue* and *Le Cri du Peuple*.

This was a *generation* which believed in the great upheavals of 1789 and 1830; a *generation* which accepted as natural the inevitable utopia spread far and wide by a popular literature which today has been erased by official literary history. We find the echo of this cult of the new, of radical rupture, in multiple texts from the period 1825–1850.

Thus we read in Ann Bignan's preface to the 1832 text entitled *L'Echafaud*[2] *(The Scaffold):*

Qu'est-il advenu depuis 1789? Cette royauté, qui ne s'était montrée jusqu'alors qu'environnée de prestiges et de respects, s'est vue contrainte de s'en aller en exil, de descendre dans les prisons, de monter sur les échafauds. La hache de 93 a, d'une part, abattu ce qui dominait, de l'autre, élevé ce qui rampait [. . .]. Les passions du peuple ont éclaté avec une **vigoureuse franchise** *et quelquefois avec une* **hideuse brutalité** *[. . .]. La révolution a dépouillé tant de vérité de* <u>leur enveloppe, que la littérature ne peut plus mentir</u> *[. . .] Si donc elle est* <u>secondée par la franche énergie des passions</u> *et* **du langage,** *elle l'est également par ces nobles principes de liberté civile et politique qui fermentent dans toutes les têtes [. . .]* [emphasis added].

(What has happened since 1789? This royalty, which had never before been seen except when surrounded by prestige and respect, found itself forced to go into exile, to descend into prison, to climb up onto the executioner's scaffold. The hatchet of 1793 has, on the one hand, slaughtered that which dominated and, on the other hand, brought up that which crawled on all fours [. . .]. The passions of the people have exploded with a **vigorous frankness** and sometimes with a **hideous brutality** [. . .]. The revolution has stripped so many <u>truths</u> of their cover, that literature <u>can no longer lie</u> [. . .]. Thus, if literature is seconded by the <u>frank energy</u> of the passions and by **language,** it is likewise seconded by those noble principles of political and civil liberty which ferment in every head [. . .].)

The Discourse of Truth

This insistence on the need for *"truth,"* for frankness, as a criterion of the new literature returns as a leitmotiv in the body of this literature which has been forgotten today. Thus, in a previous article on counter-discourse,[3] I cited the preface of an anonymous text entitled *Le dernier jour d'un employé (An Employee's Last Day)* where the author mocks Victor Hugo trying to imagine what the life of humble people is like from his comfortably bourgeois position. The author of the text proclaims,

"Mon livre est une histoire très véritable, *trop* véritable: *C'est celle de mon meilleur ami; et je ne suis qu'un historien [. . .]. Seulement, en ma qualité d'historien, je prétends au mérite de la* vérité, *de l'*exactitude *[. . .]. Il est* vrai *qu'il m'était plus facile d'y atteindre qu'à M. Hugo qui a dû se torturer l'imagination [. . .]."*

("My book is a very *true* story, too *true:* it is the story of my best friend; and

I am only an historian [. . .]. However, as an historian, I aspire to *truthfulness, precision* [. . .]. It is *true* that it was easier for me to arrive at the truth, at exactitude, than it was for Mr. Hugo who must have tortured his imagination [. . .].")

It is not surprising then that we find this same insistence on **truth** in Jules Janin's preface to *L'Ane mort et la femme guillotinée (The Dead Donkey and the Guillotined Woman)*,[4] since Joseph-Marc Bailbé, in his article *"Jules Janin et le bonheur,"*[5] attributes the anonymous text to Janin. In this preface to *L'Ane mort et la femme guillotinée*, which can justifiably be considered a major theoretical text of the nineteenth century, Janin writes,

> *Nous eûmes donc, la Critique et moi, une grande dispute sur ce qu'on appelle la vérité dans l'art. Je lui expliquais [. . .] qu'il fallait voir avant d'être vrai; que lorsqu'on avait vu, il fallait dire ce qu'on avait vu, tout ce que l'on avait vu; rien que ce qu'on avait vu; que l'art était là tout entier. [. . .] D'où il suit qu'avant de parler d'une chose il faut la voir. [. . .] Il faut en général se défier des mauvais tours de son imagination; laissez-la faire, cette folle du logis, elle va changer tout le temps [. . .]. De là résulte souvent une espèce de don quichottisme littéraire plus ridicule mille fois que tout ce que nous savions en fait d'anachronisme. Sous ce rapport, le* Don Quichotte *de Cervantès est un excellent livre peut-être, mais c'est une mauvaise action.*[6]

(We had, then, Criticism and I, a great dispute on what is called truth in art. I explained to it [. . .] that we needed to see before we could be truthful; that once we had seen, we had to say what we had seen and nothing but what we had seen and that art was completely contained therein (in what we had seen). [. . .] From which it follows that, before speaking about a thing, we must see it. [. . .] We must in general beware of the tricks of our imagination; let it do as it wishes, that crazy inhabitant of the mind, it will change all the time [. . .]. We often find, as a result of our imagination, a sort of literary quixoticism a thousand times more ridiculous than what we knew as an anachronism. In this light, Cervantès's *Don Quixote* is perhaps an excellent book, but it is a poor action.)

This campaign for truth in literature is found in writings on politics. In his work *Les Marionnettes politiques. Moeurs comtemporaines (The Political Marionnettes, Contemporary Mores)*,[7] G. Touchard-Lafosse writes,

> *Ne nous laissons pas abuser par les superficies, dans la recherche de ce qui peut plaire au public. Si je m'en rapportais aux affiches de* **cyniques révélateurs** *[. . .] si j'en croyais les organes de coteries qui proclament le succès des romans où [. . .] le peuple est représenté avec des moeurs grossières [. . .], j'écrirais des mémoires apocriphes [sic]. [. . .] Mais en perçant d'un regard moins*

bénévole l'enveloppe décevante qu'on nous montre, j'ai reconnu que le public lit avec une juste défiance *les révélations contemporaines, et qu'il n'est que médiocrement amusé par de* prétendues vérités *auxquelles il ne croit pas.*[8]

(While in search of what is pleasing to the public, let's not be taken advantage of by the superficial. If I placed my faith in the posters of **cynical revealers** [. . .] if I believed in the mouthpieces of coteries who proclaim the success of novels where [. . .] the masses are represented with crude manners [. . .], I would write apocryphal memoirs. [. . .] But by penetrating the deceptive cover that they show us with a less than benevolent eye, I realized that the public reads contemporary revelations with a *just defiance,* and that they only are only poorly amused by *alleged truths* which they don't believe.)

The argument for truth is so ubiquitous that in his preface, the editor of Auguste Ricard's novel, *La Grisette (The Young Dressmaker),*[9] makes it an essential element in his advertisement for the novel:

Ce roman offre des peintures vraies et piquantes [. . .]. [Il] reproduit avec fidélité *les moeurs faubouriennes et celles du boulevard du Temple.* Vrai *panorama, l'ouvrage que nous annonçons met en saillie ces caractères grivois si communs dans la petite propriété, et dont l'heureux type ne trouve qu'un dédaigneux accueil dans les livres d'aujourd'hui; **bégueulerie** mal entendue qui prive nos auteurs de peintures animées et* vraies.[10]

(This novel offers *true* and poignant paintings [. . .]. [It] *faithfully* reproduces the faubourien mores and those of the Temple Boulevard. A *true* panorama, the work which we are now presenting, sets in relief those risqué characters, so common among small-time proprietors; that happy type of people who in today's books have found only grudging acceptance; a misplaced prudishness (**"bégueulerie"**) which deprives our authors of *true* and animated paintings.)

The term *"bégueulerie"* (prudishness) is in italics in the original text in order to emphasize it, in order to have it be understood exactly for what it is: a popular violence done to the language. This term, which emphasizes the disgust the orthodox feel for this type of *true* literature which reproduces faithfully the faubourien mores, is therefore a veritable jewel of the popular lexicon. It has the ring of the vernacular, and returns with mockery the scorn that elegant writers affect with regard to this *true* literature. The term *bégueulerie* is "popular" in a superlative manner, since three rules on the formation of polished French are transgressed here. The word is first of all an agglutination of two terms—a technique that is formally prohibited in French and defined by Thomas and Darmesteter as the prototype of popular lexical formation. It is also a transgression of the classic rule for the placement of adjectives which states that "the known precedes the unknown": Here, the adjective *"bée"* (open) precedes the noun *"gueule"* (animal's mouth, or mouth). Finally, it is the substitution of the popular term *"gueule"* (for the more familiar term *"bouche"* (mouth). To be *"bégueule"* in popular speech is to remain *"bouche bée"* (open-mouthed) from disgust when faced with something abject. If, in 1830, "respectable" authors stand agape before writings which reproduce *truthfully* the popular mores, the situation seems hardly to have changed in 1870. We find the same *bégueulerie* in the words of the Goncourt brothers when the Paris Commune triumphs: *"Risum teneatis!* Jules Vallès is the minister of Public Education. The Bohemian of the cafés now occupies Villemain's seat!"

This echo was repeated in the halls of Versailles; in addition to the *ultra* Maxime du Camp, we can cite Paul de Saint-Victor who wrote: *"Un bâtard de Marat, Jules Vallès, dans* Le Cri du Peuple, *vociférait la haine et la rage. Bohème des lettres, aigri par une jeunesse misérable, affolé d'orgueil, altéré d'envie, sa poche à fiel crevée s'était répandue dans son style. [. . .] L'incendiaire couvait sous l'énergumène illettré."*[11] ("One of Marat's bastards, Jules Vallès, in the *Cri du Peuple*, spews out his hatred and rage. A Bohemian of letters, embittered by an impoverished youth, maddened by pride, altered by envy, his bag of malice has split open and has spilled out onto his style. [. . .] The incendiary was smouldering inside the illiterate fanatic.")

As for George Sand, who the Goncourt brothers said *"rêvait de sauter sur les genoux de Robespierre"* ("dreamed of jumping on Robespierre's lap"), despite the influence of her socialist mentors, Michel de Bourges, Lamennais and Pierre Leroux—of whom she claimed to be the disciple—she writes, *"Le mouvement a été organisé par des hommes [. . .] mus par la haine, l'ambition déçue, le patriotisme mal entendu, le fanatisme sans idéal, la niaiserie du sentiment ou la méchanceté naturelle."*[12] ("The movement was organized by men [. . .] moved by hatred, by disappointed ambition, by misunderstood patriotism, by fanaticism without ideals, by the foolishness of feelings, or by natural maliciousness.")

In 1870, then, Vallès pays the price for standing out amidst the gray mediocrity of his generation: Arrested, emprisoned, and on the run, he has to take the road to exile in London like many other marginal writers who had tied the destiny of a *true* new literature to revolutionary adventurism.

Thus, in 1985 or 1989, to glorify the republican spirit and the revolutionary ideal in Victor Hugo is to celebrate a well-off writer who has become popular, and to ignore Jules Vallès is to neglect a writer who made the mistake of not leaving the popular register in order to become popular.

So as to introduce the question which interests me, that is, what are the theoretical stakes implicated in the definition of discursive revolutionary aesthetics in the literature of the nineteenth century, I chose to illustrate the debate by emblematizing it with these two figures: Victor Hugo and Jules Vallès. Like Philippe Bonnefis, I could have opposed the renowned writer Zola to the discredited writer Vallès, since *Germinal* has been acknowledged for some time now as, to use a now consecrated term, a "*roman* anti-peuple" (*anti-people* novel). Claude Duchet, among others, has demonstrated this aspect of *Germinal*. Duchet emphasizes the fact that we find the word "worker" with a pejorative meaning when not used with a positive qualification. Paul Lidsky[13] also supports this view by affirming that Zola found a way to ward off his past fears of the Commune by writing in *Germinal*:

> *"C'était la vision rouge de la révolution qui les emportait tous fatalement, par une soirée sanglante de cette fin-de-siècle. Oui, un soir, le peuple lâché, débridé, galoperait ainsi sur les chemins; et il ruisselerait le sang des bourgeois, ils promèneraient des têtes, ils sèmeraient l'or des coffres éventrés. Les femmes hurleraient, les hommes auraient ces machoires de loups, ouvertes pour mordre."[14]*

> ("And what they saw was a red vision of the coming revolution that would inevitably carry them all off one bloody night at the end of this epoch. Yes, one night the people would break loose and hurtle like this along the roads, dripping with bourgeois blood, waving severed heads, and scattering gold from rifled safes. The women would yell and the men's teeth would be bared like the jaws of wolves ready to bite.")

It doesn't really matter then which emblematic figures are chosen to dramatize the alternative; in the reevaluation of literary canons, it is most important to verify the simultaneous existence of two discourses which claim to be socially revolutionary. Of these, one is artificial, manufactured, and commonly accepted as a replacement for reality in literary production, and, for that reason, usurps the place of the original discourse, whose expression while *true* and immediate, is also socially inacceptable and therefore unusable as a literary commodity.

All discussions about the problems imposed by this state of affairs must avoid focusing on the simple question of legitimacy; it is of little importance today whether or not Hugo or Zola, writers described as "bourgeois," did or did not have the right to appropriate popular speech. The analysis of this type of discourse must first of all identify and define the discursive characteristics which established it and then must recognize the epistemological terrain from which it originates. To admit the possibility that one can define the characteristics of a revolutionary-popular discourse presupposes automatically the existence of a model of reference and of a restrictive configuration of analytic criteria.

These writerly characteristics are in large part dependent on an aesthetic doctrine of *language*. The term "aesthetic" is not taken here in its Kantian sense, that is, it is not tied to the perception of the work of art and does not refer therefore to a "judgment in taste," but rather it implies a body of principles which are related to the process of the production of discourse.

The philosophical and literary ideas which surface during the years 1830–1850 determine the historical criteria. In 1827, *La Palingénésie Sociale* by Ballanche, the beginning of Michelet's translation of Vico's *Scienza Nuova*, and, in the newspaper *Le Globe*, Jouffroy's comparative study of Vico and Herder all appear simultaneously. These publications, marked by a common reference to Herder and Vico, set up the boundaries for my work on literary discourse of revolutionary inspiration, to the extent that a double opposition is elaborated here that we can summarize as: "spontaneism" versus intellectualism and *sign* versus *symbol*. In his *Traité sur l'origine de la Langue (Treatise on the Origins of Language)*, Herder takes up Rousseau's theses on the merit of the *state of nature* and the quality of the *pre-social* and *pre-civil* state of humanity. Linguistic phenomena are reinterpreted in order to serve as a foundation for a comparative anthropology in which literature is indissociable from its popular origins: This is the basis for the concept of *folklore* and, more generally, of philology. As a corollary to this union between language and popular literature in its primitive forms, Herder makes himself the spokesman for the *symbol*, as opposed to the *sign*. As Todorov notes in the chapter *"La crise romantique"* ("Romantic Crisis") in his work *Théories du Symbole (Theories of the Symbol)*,[15] Herder pursues Rousseau's ideas and argues in favor of the symbol as a privileged mode of expression for an original tropological language. The minimal unit of meaning to retain is not the *sign*, which has a transitive meaning founded on convention (the sign represents something for someone), rather this minimal unit is the *symbol*, which has intransitive meaning (the thing signifies something in itself). In the years 1825–1850, we therefore see appearing in France a literary and philosophical current which valorizes the *symbol* as a mode of discursive creation in which a coincidence between the designator and the designated, between the expression and the natural, is marked. The counterpart, of course, is the rejection of the disjunction or the difference that the *sign* introduces between the thing and its designation. This critique of the *sign* explains the virulence of the attack that Michelet launches in *Le Peuple*[16] (The People), against false men of genius, the true scholars: *"Logiciens sans métaphysique, légistes moins le droit et l'histoire, ils ne croient qu'aux signes, aux formes, et à la phrase. En toute chose, il leur manque la substance, la vie et le sentiment de la vie, ces terribles abstracteurs de quintessence s'arment de cinq ou six formules qui [. . .] leur servent à abstraire les hommes."* ("Logicians without metaphysics, jurists without law or history, they only believe in *signs*, in *forms*, and in the *sentence*. In all things they lack substance, life, and the feeling for life; these horrible abstractors of quintessences arm themselves with five or six formulas which [. . .] serve to isolate men.")

Underlying this opposition to the sign slides the primordial and radical critique that *writers of the true* address to the "great authors." In their writings, these celebrated authors transgress the law of the true word. The emphasis on elements borrowed from the popular domain in a discourse which does not adopt them, which does not take them in and note them as vignettes of the real, exposes the illusory nature of the pragmatic conditions of literary enunciation. The organization of syntagmatic narrative is not what is challenged, but rather the criteria for the meta-verification of the discourse. By contamination, the status of the subject of enunciation is also subject to challenge. The locus of truth for the author as well as his rapport of experience to the represented real are questioned in these writings of revolutionary literature.

In between the lines of this type of writing—which promotes adherence to the supported cause and the authentic coincidence of the author with his/her discourse—we find the theory of *"alethic"* language, founded on the principle of organic integrity of the *symbol*. The *truth of a discourse* exists only in so far as the discourse and the represented thing support a necessary relationship of natural homogeneity. "Elegant" writers diffuse and postulate an aesthetic founded on the separation of the *sign* and thus place themselves, by statute, on the side of the discursive duplicity of writing, since the relation between the *sign* and the thing is, by definition, non-motivated, unverifiable and constantly deferred. The political and literary revolution begins with a restitution of authentic discourse.

Sign and Symbol

Once we have completed this bold analysis and moved beyond the satisfaction of having reduced a complex question to a clear dichot-

omy, preconceived, preestablished, sign versus symbol, what emerges
is a moment of discontent.

When, for the purpose of my demonstration, I choose to understand the term *sign* as Michelet used it in *Le Peuple* as the exact
equivalent of the contemporary concept of *sign*, I commit, for the sake
of critical expediency, an anachronism which compromises the very
value of my analysis. The *sign* that Michelet reproaches the intellec-
tuals of his time for favoring is the *sign* of the Port-Royal grammarians,
that is, a *sign* that is *rational* and *abstract*. Today, the only grammarian
we could find who would refer to that type of sign would be Chomsky.
Michelet's *sign* belongs to a discussion on the impact of experience, on
the "restitution of life itself" and not to a discussion on the *truth* of
representation.

As André Chervel, in his study *"Le débat sur l'arbitraire du signe au
XIXe siècle"* ("The Debate on the Arbitrariness of the Sign of the
Nineteenth Century"), indicates, the debate over the nature of the
sign such as we know it today began only in 1880–1900, well after
Michelet's death. Eventually, this debate in one of these forms, lead to
the elementary dichotomy between *symbol* and *sign* which has served
as my thesis during the investigation so far. But this opposition is not
universally valid; it is marked and dated. To be precise, it appears in
1916, in the first part of Saussure's posthumous work *Cours de Linguistique Générale (Course on General Linguistics)*: **"On s'est servi du**
mot symbole *pour désigner le signe linguistique, ou plus exactement ce que
nous appelons le signifiant. Il y a des inconvénients à l'admettre, justement
à cause de notre premier principe [de l'arbitraire]. Le symbole a pour
caractère de n'être jamais tout à fait arbitraire; it n'est pas vide, il y a un
rudiment de lien naturel entre le signifiant et le signifié"* ("**We used** the
word symbol to designate the linguistic sign, or to be more precise,
what we call the signifier. There are inconveniences in allowing this,
specifically because of our first principle [of the arbitrary]. The symbol's character is never completely arbitrary; it is not empty, there is a
rudiment of natural linking between the signifier and the signified.")[17]

Saussure, or his disciples, write: *"On s'est servi du"* ("**We
used . . .**"); using the past optative mode in French. The fact is that
today this fundamental distinction between *sign* and *symbol*, relayed by
structuralism, serves to characterize the French model of the study of
the sign that we know as *semiology*. In the Anglo-Saxon world of
studies of the sign, we *still use ("on se sert toujours de")*, interchangea-
bly, the terms *symbol* and *sign*. In this context, then, to define the
alethic character of revolutionary discourse as participating in an
aesthetic of the *symbol* does not at all imply that the alternative would

be an aesthetic of the *sign*. The alethic specificity of revolutionary discourse must therefore be formulated in a universally valid aesthetic framework which would include any symbol or any sign.

For those who are inspired by semiotic Vulgate, it is now well established that the world of sign study is divided between researchers who on the one hand use the Saussurian type of sign revised by Hjelmslev, and on the other hand researchers who prefer Frege's tripartite sign, reworked by Charles Peirce, modified by Mukarovsky, and finally popularized by Ogden and Richards in 1923. In good terminological ethics, *semiotics* is the Peircian theory of signs, and *semiology* is the Saussurian theory of signs.

On an extremely schematic level, then, it looks as though the opposition between these two sign theories arises primarily with regard to two aspects of the sign—its nature (binary or ternary) and its field of application (language or the world).

In a short essay I haven't the time to enter into the details of these distinctions, so I will content myself with simply suggesting that this neat opposition which the Vulgate has proposed is incomplete and does not truly allow for a discussion of the methodological conditions of the applicability of these two types of sign to a problematic of revolutionary discourse. Or, at the least, I will suggest that the opposition which the Vulgate proposes obscures another opposition which appears to me to be not only more productive but more likely to bring about a fundamental theoretical reflection on this type of revolutionary discourse.

To choose the Saussurian sign is to abandon oneself to a *hermeneutic of indetermination*, whereas to choose the Peircian sign is to allow oneself to believe in a *hermeneutic of discovery*. Behind this opposition, a metaphysical dimension quite naturally takes shape and, in order to understand where the theoretical stake of the definition of revolutionary discourse is located, two texts by Peirce (still not translated into French) are fundamental. I am thinking specifically of "Lesson from the History of Philosophy. 1. Nominalism" which opens the *Collected Papers* and the very important "Critical Review of Berkeley's Idealism" which, together with "Scholastic Realism," constitute the central philosophical section of the conferences on pragmatism.[18]

What can we retain from his text on Berkeley? First of all, Peirce's interest in this English philosopher is related to the fact that, unlike many philosophers of his time, Berkeley was not at all influenced by Descartes. This consideration in itself is anecdotal and touches only French pride, because, as we know, via André Glucksman, "Descartes is France." But we must read on.

Realism

Peirce affirms that, for him, the history of philosophy, at least since the Middle Ages, is dominated by two competing currents of thought: nominalism and realism. He writes against the nominalist current which he recognizes as dominating his era through various movements such as phenomenalism, individualism, and materialism. The entire distinction between nominalism and realism is based on conditions for the perception of reality, and Peirce explicitly asserts his adherence to the *realist* current. For him, nominalism, which takes up the traditional scholastic opposition *in re* / *in voce* and places on the one side the object in the world and on the other side the element of language which represents it, is unproductive because there is no thing-in-itself. There exists only the *true mental perception of the real*. Peirce writes, "Realist theory is completely fatal to the idea that there can exist a thing-in-itself—a thing which would exist independently from the conception that the mind has of it."[19] To be brief, I want to point out that, for Peirce, there exists only a perceived and mental reality, and that this individual perception is what constitutes *his model of the sign*.

Because there is no object in Peirce's realist theory other than that taken in the semiosis of the sign, the question of the *truth* of the object is plainly situated in the refinement of the semiotic operation, and the object cannot have any exterior existence of its own. The truth of the object is the domain of the perceptible and can only be affirmed in the completeness of the sign as a teleological figure.

From a semiotic point of view, it is therefore perfectly clear that the revolutionary discourse of the nineteenth century, with its demands for *truth* and its call for direct experience, is faithfully inscribed in the epistemological schema of the Peircian sign with its realist origins. This sign postulates, *in fine*, the existence of a truth of meaning whose duty is to be universal and irreducible to a collection of individual opinions. In this immediate perception of the real, through our actual experience, we find the demands of *adherence* and *immediate participation*, which, in the revolutionary discourse of the nineteenth century, prevail as a guarantee of truth.

Finally, it is useful to reiterate that, by bringing back the realism / nominalism opposition, we restore to the misused term of *realism* its proper etymological meaning. In its first scholastic definition, the term serves to define the immediate and true experience of a reality which is external to the subject; the term conserves this definition in the Anglo-Saxon world, and the *"realismus"* of German authors from the beginning of the 19th century (such as Herweg and Beck) is charged with revolutionary pathos. In 1798 (dictionaries agree on this date) the term becomes part of the philosophical vocabulary and, during this revolutionary period, it still retains its technical, scholastic definition. In 1833, we see the term appear as a literary label in Gaston Planche's work and it is obvious that at this time, in this meaning of the word, it still contains the elements which attach it to its philosophical meaning and to its tradition of *true* speech.

The conflict of *Truth* and *Beauty,* which appears in the poetic aesthetic of the middle of the nineteenth century, progressively tips interests toward *Beauty.* This is why, in the *Salon of 1859,* Baudelaire is able to write, *"La passion exclusive du vrai [. . .] opprime et réduit le goût pour le Beau"* ("The exclusive passion for truth [. . .] oppresses and reduces the taste for the beautiful.") It is true that in *"Le Mauvais Vitrier"* ("The Bad Glazier") and *"Le Vieux Saltimbanque"* ("The Old Acrobat") from *Petits Poèmes en prose (Short Prose Poems),* the worldly man only perceives Parisian street talk as *"un cri perçant, discordant"* ("a piercing, discordant cry").

In the *Dictionnaire* by Thomas and Darmesteter (1889)[20] the term realism only means *"Reproduction de la réalité avec ce qu'elle peut avoir de laid et de vulgaire"* ("Reproduction of reality with its ugly or vulgar aspects"). It is this meaning that has been promulgated by the *Dictionnaire* of the Académie since 1878. To take up Bignan's terms once again, we find here not *"vigoureuse franchise"* ("vigorous frankness"), but *"la hideuse brutalité"* ("hideous brutality"). This is still more or less what we find today in the *Petit Robert* dictionary,[21] except with a higher degree of oversight, *"Réalisme: Conception de la littérature, de l'art, selon laquelle l'artiste ne doit pas chercher à idéaliser le réel ou à en donner une image épurée"* ("Realism: a conception of literature, of art, according to which the artist must not try to idealize the real or to give it a purified image"). The list of antonyms that we find following this definition is in itself significant because of the omissions it chooses to make: *"Idéalisme, immatérialisme, fantastique, irréalisme")* ("Idealism, immaterialism, the fantastic, irrealism"). We search in vain for the term which *a contrario* founded conceptually the term *realism: nominalism.*

Today, the trace of the oppositions has disappeared and "realism" is given simply as the opposite of "idealism," thus reducing the choice to a judgment of taste between a beautiful representation and an abject representation. The demands of *Truth,* of teleological sanction, which is, as I hope I have shown, at the center of the constitution of an aesthetic of revolutionary discourse, have let themselves be crushed by the *empire* of linguistic signs which are the basic units of semiotics, a discipline, according to Umberto Eco's now famous saying, *"studying everything which can be used in order to lie."*[22]

Notes

1. Philippe Bonnefis, Valles: *Du bon usage de la lame et de l'aiguille* (Lausanne: l'Age d'Homme, 1982), 13.

2. Ann Bignan, *L'Echafaud* (Paris: Bichet, 1832), 12.

3. Jean-Jacques Thomas, "Langue populaire/Littérature populaire," *Poétique*, 37 (1979): 10–23.

4. Anonyme [Jules Janin], *L'Ane mort et la femme guillotinée* (Paris: Baudouin, 1829).

5. Joseph-Marc Bailbé, *"Jules Janin et le bonheur,"* in *Jules Janin et son temps: un moment du romantisme* (Paris: Presses Universitaires de France, 1974), 41–57.

6. *L'Ane mort et la femme guillotinée*, op. cit., 18–19.

7. G. Touchard-Lafosse, *Les Marionnettes politiques. Moeurs contemporaines* (Paris: Renduel, 1829). Touchard-Lafosse also wrote *L'Habit de Chambellan, Le Lutin,* and *Le Précis de l'histoire de Napoléon.*

8. *Les Marionnettes politiques*, op. cit, XI–XII.

9. August Ricard, *La Grisette* (Paris: Tétot, Lecointe, Corbet, 1829).

10. Ibid., I–III.

11. P. de Saint-Victor, *Barbares et bandits* (Paris: Lévy, 1872), 246.

12. George Sand, *Réponse à un ami*, in *Le Temps* (October 3, 1871).

13. Paul Lidsky, *Les Ecrivains contre la Commune* (Paris: Maspéro, 1982), 114.

14. Emile Zola, *Germinal* (Paris: Fasquelle, 1928), 364–5. The translation below is by Leonard Tancock, from the Penguin edition of Zola's novel (Middlesex: Harmondsworth, 1954), 334–35.

15. Tzvetan Todorov, *Théories du symbole* (Paris: Seuil, 1977), 179–260.

16. Jules Michelet, *Le Peuple*, in *L'Humanité en marche*, (Paris: Editions du Burin, 1971), 264.

17. Ferdinand de Saussure, *Cours de Linguistique Générale*, Tullio de Mauro, ed. (Paris: Payot, 1972), 101.

18. Charles S. Peirce, *Collected Papers of Charles Sanders Peirce*, eds. C. Hartshorne and P. Weiss (Cambridge: Harvard University Press, 1931–1935).

19. Philip P. Wiener, ed., *Charles S. Peirce: Selected Writings* (New York: Dover, 1958), 82.

20. Arsène Darmesteter, A. Hatzfeld, A. Thomas, *Dictionnaire général de la langue française* (Paris: Delagrave, 1889), Vol. II, 1880.

21. Paul Robert, *Le Petit Robert* (Paris: Le Robert, 1988), 1617.

22. Umberto Eco, *A Theory of Semiotics* (Bloomington: Indiana University Press, 1979), 7.

Le Plissement and la fêlure: The Paris Commune in Vallès's L'Insurgé and Zola's La Débâcle

CHARLES J. STIVALE

In his provocative analysis of Zola's *La Bête humaine* in *The Logic of Sense*, Gilles Deleuze develops the bipolar oscillation which occurs in Zola's work between the *la petite hérédité des instincts* ("small heredity of instincts") and the *la grande hérédité* ("grand heredity"), both of *la fêlure* ("the fissure") and of the *l'Instinct de mort* ("death Instinct").[1] According to this model, the instincts alone seem to drive the subject's actions in the case of Jacques Lantier's love for Séverine which apparently palliates the effects of the hereditary *fêlure*. But, at the same time, says Deleuze, *la fêlure* "is actualized in each body in relation to the instincts which open a way for it, sometimes mending it a little, sometimes widening it, up to the final shattering" (*LS* pp. 325; 378). Thus, in yielding to the silent "death Instinct" by killing Séverine, Jacques returns to the death from which their love had originally sprung, then finally succumbs himself to the "death Instinct" embodied by the "epic symbol" of the train (*LS* p. 332; 385). It is tempting to extend this bipolar model to other novels by Zola as does Deleuze briefly for *Thérèse Raquin, L'Assommoir*, and *Nana*, and in this essay, I propose to examine Zola's presentation of the Paris Commune in *La Débâcle* in light of *la fêlure*,[2] and then to consider a different depiction of this event, from Vallès's *L'Insurgé*, with an alternate model of analysis, what Deleuze calls *le plissement* ("folding") in his recent study entitled *Foucault*.[3]

With the term *plissement*, Deleuze designates a mode of comprehending the process of subjectivation, or assemblage of the subject, from two perspectives. Conceived not only in terms of the concurrent dimensions of knowledge, power, and thought, this process also posits the imbrication of "inside" and "outside"—"the inside *of* the outside," says Deleuze, insofar as "the outside is not a fixed limit but a moving matter animated by peristaltic movements, folds and foldings that together make up an inside" (*F* pp. 96–97; 103–104). Deleuze explains how, in Foucault's work, the dualism on the level of knowledge, i.e., between the visual and the articulable, exists as a form of exteriority and dispersion, two multiplicities that "open up onto a third: a multiplicity of relations between forces, a multiplicity of diffusion which no longer splits into two and is free of any dualizable form" (*F* pp. 83–84; 90). It is the interior/exterior functioning of the dimensions of knowledge, power, and thought that the mode of *le plissement* brings into perspective, and by juxtaposing the Commune episodes in *La Débâcle* and *L'Insurgé*, I wish to examine two distinct ways in which the fictional subject is constituted through contrasting modes of textualizing history.

As David Baguley has shown in his study of focalization in the *le récit de guerre* ("the war tale"),[4] the final chapters of *La Débâcle* stand in sharp opposition to the sections that precede them; that is, until their escape from the prison camp following the defeat at Sedan, the focal protagonists, Jean Macquart and Maurice Levasseur, are united in their participation in the hereditary paroxysms of the final days of the decrepit Second Empire. Subsequently, however, *la fêlure* operates an abrupt bifurcation with their disunion into different narrative and psychosocial directions. In the terms of Deleuze's analysis in *The Logic of Sense*, the "small heredity" functions in Jean Macquart throughout the novel, generally, as he leads his platoon in the struggle within the military institution of the State apparatus. More specifically, he creates a lasting bond with the previously dissolute Maurice and thereby guides him through an ordeal in which the "grand heredity of *la fêlure*" is displaced temporarily from Maurice's unstable character and is textualized historically in the crumbling Second Empire and embodied in the decaying personage of Napoléon III. But, the bifurcation of Maurice's near disappearance for several chapters into Paris, while Jean recuperates at Remilly, results in a shift in the hereditary matrix: the "small heredity of instincts" emerges, on one hand, with Jean's will to reenlist in the military apparatus and blind allegiance to the apparently "healing" force which the Versailles government comes to embody and enact. On the other hand, the "small heredity" directs Maurice's alienation from the military apparatus and his *détraquement* ("breakdown") in Paris progressively towards the "death Instinct" of the "grand heredity" as he is swept, as it were, into the historical undertow of the increasingly deranged oppositional forces which conquer and then defend the city throughout the Commune.

In order to resolve this conflict of the "small heredity" in its search for an object, Zola must resort to the device of the two chance encounters of Jean and Maurice in the streets of Paris. The first one culminates in a decisive schism:

Tous deux restèrent quelques secondes face à face, [Maurice] dans l'exaspération du coup de démence qui emportait Paris entier, ce mal venu de loin, des ferments mauvais du dernier règne, [Jean] fort de son bon sens et de son ignorance, sain encore d'avoir poussé à part, dans la terre du travail et de l'épargne. (D p. 871)

("They both remained staring at each other for several seconds, [Maurice] in the exasperation of the mad impulse that was overwhelming all of Paris, the sickness brought from afar, the bad ferment of the previous reign, [Jean] fortified by his good sense and his ignorance, still healthy from having grown up elsewhere, in the land of toil and thrift.")

But this incompatibility, not so much ideological, suggests Sandy Petrey, as "the contrast . . . between two states of health,"[5] fails to dislodge them from their mutually fraternal embrace:

Tous les deux étaient frères pourtant, un lien solide les attachait, et ce fut un acharnement, lorsque, soudain, une bousculade qui se produisit, les sépara. (D p. 871)

("However, both of them were brothers, a solid bond held them together, and it was a desperate moment when, suddenly, a commotion which arose separated them.")

This dislocation of fraternity and the slide toward *la fêlure* occur only through a second chance encounter, prepared by and within the historical momentum of the "grand heredity" during *la Semaine sanglante* (the "Bloody Week," May 21–28, 1871). Maurice passes through successive states dominated by *ce rêve fou* ("this mad dream") of Paris's destruction (*D.* pp. 876), by the emotional and physical *ivresse* ("inebriation") on the barricades (*D* pp. 877–882), then by "a doubt" (*D* p. 881) and *une nausée* ("a sickness") (*D* p. 882) produced when he recognizes a former soldier from Sedan, the opportunistic Chouteau, now a fellow *communard* setting the city ablaze. These reflections before the conflagration and destruction of Paris lead Maurice to the edge of *la fêlure* and the "death Instinct" with his conclusion delivered via the indirect mode: "If he had made a mistake, at least let him pay for his error with his own blood!" (*D* p. 881).[6] However, the *communards'* opposition also sweeps Jean, despite his often-mentioned "good peasant sense," into the same maelstrom of the "grand heredity":

Le récit des abominations de la Commune . . . le jetaient hors de lui, blessant son respect de la propriété et son besoin d'ordre. . . . Les incendies étaient venus l'affoler. . . . Et lui dont les exécutions sommaires, la veille, avaient serré le coeur, ne s'appartenait plus, farouche, les yeux hors de la tête, tapant, hurlant. (*D* p. 883)

("The story of the Commune's abominations . . . drove him beyond himself, wounding his respect for property and his need for order. . . . The fires came to madden him,. . . . And although the summary executions the previous evening had wrenched his heart, he could no longer control himself, now savage, his eyes bulging, striking, screaming.")

The collision of instinct with its object and the dislocation of fraternity are prepared, as Deleuze suggests, "in relations between temperaments which are always stretched out over" *la fêlure* (*LS* pp. 323; 375) in the fatal encounter that Naomi Schor calls their "dysphoric reunion":[7]

> *Ce fut sous la poussée furieuse du destin, [Jean] courut, il cloua l'homme sur la barricade, d'un coup de baïonnette. Maurice n'avait pas eu le temps de se retourner. Il jeta un cri, il releva la tête. . . . 'Oh! Jean, mon vieux Jean, est-ce toi?"* (*D* p. 883)

("It was under a furious thrust of fate that [Jean] ran, impaling the man on the barricade with a stab of his bayonet. Maurice did not have the time to turn around. He let out a cry, lifted his head. . . . 'Oh! Jean, my friend Jean, is it you?' ")

Throughout the episodes preceding and following Sedan, Maurice has served for Jean as "the Same," that is, a brother-in-arms and would-be brother-in-law, given the growing relationship between Jean and Maurice's sister, Henriette.[8] But, in the paroxysm of the Commune and of the "death Instinct," this "Same" becomes "the Other," Maurice as *ce lettré* ("this educated man") transformed into "an instinctive being" (*D* p. 860) possessed by "a blind need for vengeance and destruction" (*D* p. 868). Just as Jacques must kill Séverine in *La Bête humaine,* Deleuze suggests, "in order for the small heredity to link up with the grand, and for all the instincts to enter" *la fêlure* (*LS* pp. 329; 381), Jean must also kill Maurice. But this death coincides with a transformed model of *la fêlure* as presented in the dénouement, for Maurice's individual "breakdown," his commitment to the final gasp of the Second Empire's "death Instinct" through the Commune, yields to Jean's cataclysmic vision of the necessity for national healing, rebirth and return to order which Zola depicts in the final lines:

Le champ ravagé était en friche, la maison brûlée était parterre; et Jean, le plus humble et le plus douloureux, s'en alla, marchant à l'avenir, à la grande et rude besogne de toute une France à refaire. (D p. 912)

("The ravaged field lay fallow, the burned house was flattened; and Jean, the most humble and afflicted man, moved on, walking toward the future, toward the great and difficult task of remaking all of France.")

While the depiction of historical events in *La Débâcle* is eventually supplanted by Zola's mythology of *la fêlure*, Vallès quite effectively depicts another mode of existence in revolt, Jacques Vingtras's life in the process of *plissement* ("folding"). This process, which Deleuze links in Foucault's work to the theme of the double, consists of "an interiorization of the outside," a redoubling of the Other, a repetition of the Different: "It is never the other who is a double in the doubling process, it is a self that lives in me as the double of the other: I do not encounter myself on the outside, I find the other in me" (*F* pp. 98; 105). This operation which, says Deleuze, "resembles exactly the invagination of a tissue in embryology, or the act of doubling in sewing" (*F* pp. 98; 105), recalls the incessant struggle between Jacques Vingtras and his mother in *L'Enfant*, which Philippe Bonnefis has discussed by studying Madame Vingtras's efforts on behalf of Jacques—to wash him, to feed him, to control his comportment, and most notably, to dress him—and thereby to "divide herself or to double herself in him: *("se dédouble[r] ou se redouble[r] en lui")*.[9]

Furthermore, the context of Greek life to which Deleuze refers in his reflection on Foucault's *L'Usage des plaisirs* is entirely appropriate regarding Jacques Vingtras, whose father endorses fully the "classic" regime of strengthening through suffering to which a colleague, the professor Bergougnard, submits his children:

Il rossait les siens au nom de Sparte et de Rome—Sparte les jours de gifles, et Rome les jours de fessées. (E p. 246)[10]

("He would whip his children in the name of Sparta and Rome, Sparta on the days of slapping and Rome on the days of spanking.")

For Deleuze emphasizes the importance of what Foucault calls a " 'relation to oneself' that consciously derives from one's relations with others" and a " 'self-constitution' that consciously derives from the moral code as a rule for knowledge" (*F* pp. 100; 107). In the Trilogy, these constitutive relations emerge at the end of *L'Enfant* and struggle for independence in the period preceding and following 1848 in *Le*

Bachelier. "It is as if," says Deleuze, "the relations of the outside folded back to create a doubling, allow a relation to oneself to emerge, and constitute an inside which is hollowed out and develops its own unique dimension" (*F* pp. 100; 107), that is, "a dimension of subjectivity derived from power and knowledge, without being dependent on them" (*F* pp. 101; 109). For Jacques Vingtras, this process of resistance is an assemblage of words, images, concepts, and propositions in which the subject constitutes the locus of a continuous life experimentation that escapes the line of death (in *Le Bachelier*), first during the events of 1848, then in the years of difficult economic survival under the Second Empire. Prepared by these bitter experiences and by his growing commitment to oppositional journalism and writing (in the first half of *L'Insurgé*), Vingtras faces the Commune as a subject traversed by the pressures and the constitution of *le plissement*, situated by history as it positions both the subject-group of the *bacheliers* transformed into insurgents, and their struggle with subjugation, i.e., with the "unfolding," by conflicting forces of power from outside and within the group (*F* pp. 103; 110).[11] Yet, Vingtras maintains a "relation to himself" by exerting a force of resistance, "the outside" as "opening on to a future: nothing ends, since nothing has begun, but everything is transformed" (*F* pp. 89; 95).

   This process of subjectivation is textualized, on a molar level, by the various subject positions which Vingtras assumes during the conflictual *plissement* of the Commune depicted in *L'Insurgé*'s second half. Having been forced into hiding in February, 1871, following his condemnation for participating in the 31 October 1870 attempted coup, Vingtras can return to activity with his credibility doubly reinforced. Not only was he also condemned for signing *l'Affiche rouge* in January, thereby openly opposing the so-called "Government of National Defense," but as editor of *Le Cri du peuple*, he is empowered to proclaim the political import of the Communal insurrection, presented through Vallès's own editorial of March 28, 1871, reprinted in chapter XXVI and attributed to Jacques Vingtras:

'*Quoiqu'il arrive, dussions-nous être de nouveau vaincus et mourir demain, notre génération est consolée! Nous sommes payés de vingt ans de défaites et d'angoisses. . . . Et toi, marmot, qui joues aux billes derrière la barricade, viens que je t'embrasse aussi! . . . Nous avons saigné et pleuré pour toi. Tu recueilleras notre héritage. Fils des désespérés, tu seras un homme libre.*' (*I* p. 253)

("Whatever happens, even if we must be defeated again and die tomorrow, our generation is consoled! We are paid back for twenty years of defeats and agony. . . . And you, kid, playing marbles behind the barricade, come let me hug you too! . . . We have bled and cried for you. You will reap our heritage. Son of desperate men, you will be a free man.")

Vingtras affirms his insurgent activity further as popular delegate from the *XVe arrondissement* to the Commune's "Central Committee"; as mediator throughout the Commune in internal struggles between *communards* of differing radical stripes; and as committed partisan during *la Semaine sanglante;* then outlaw from the Versailles government in his flight into exile. But this triumphant political stance is nonetheless tempered by Vingtras's continuing "self-constitution" (i.e., the articulation of an alternate moral code) and by his concomitant "relation to oneself" of resistance. This dual process of subjectivation can be seen in the numerous moments of reflection in which Vingtras humbly recognizes his own limits in the various subject positions, and even the very limits of the insurrectional possibilities, but also maintains a firm commitment to his chosen path.

Furthermore, this process of subjectivation is textualized on a molecular level, in terms of the mediating role fulfilled by Jacques Vingtras as "author function," for example, in the system of nomination developed throughout *L'Insurgé*.[12] While toponyms abound in Zola's meticulous description of the events during and following Sedan, he barely mentions the historical agents of the Commune at all, limiting his references to four *communards* responsible for the military defense (*D* pp. 876, 879), and privileging instead the proponents of the Versailles government. At one point, in fact, the narrator reveals himself behind Maurice's ruminations:

A la vérité *après les élections, les noms des membres de la Commune l'avaient un peu surpris par l'extraordinaire mélange de modérés, de révolutionnaires, de socialistes de toutes sectes, à qui la grande oeuvre se trouvait confiée.* (*D* p. 874)

("*In truth*," the narrator insists, "after the elections, the names of the members of the Commune had surprised him somewhat by the extraordinary mix of moderates, revolutionaries, socialists of all stripes, to whom the great task was confided,") (my emphasis).

This appeal to *la vérité* ("truth") indicates the author's commitment to depicting only a particular form of justice, and the next sentence is barely credible as issuing from Maurice's focalization, given his limited revolutionary experience in Paris since his arrival in November: "He knew several of these men, he judged them to be quite mediocre" (*D* p. 874).

Zola generally refers to the crowd of *communards* as collective agent with the metonymical toponym, "Paris," and this would seem to correspond to what Naomi Schor has identified as the "double crowd structure" in *La Débâcle*, the collective agent of "macroconflict" constituting the locus of "the central microconflict of the novel, the one opposing Jean to Maurice."[13] In *L'Insurgé*, by contrast, the only agent to maintain a fictional name is Vingtras, from whose perspective the actual participants in the historical events are presented in detail, frankly criticized or exalted, but all put into an active, dispersed play of agents in diverse subject positions.[14] Situated within this nominative *plissement*, the fictional name "Jacques Vingtras" does not function as simple title or form of ridicule as in *L'Enfant* and *Le Bachelier*. In *L'Insurgé*, this name also coincides with a multiplicity of subject positions, for example, as a form of self-address, as formula of reproach and of praise, and as the locus of oscillation regarding the strength of commitment to the Commune. A crucial example occurs during the street fighting of *la Semaine sanglante*, in chapter XXXII, entitled *Les Incendies* ("The Fires"). Beseeched by "a dairymaid who had extended me credit" to oppose the strategy of conflagration, Vingtras pauses "in a tête-à-tête with myself for a moment." But rather than slide into a suicidal abyss as does Maurice at the sight of Chouteau, thereby refusing any subjectivation in his flight toward the "death Instinct," Vingtras returns to the fray, proclaiming, "It's all thought out! I'm staying with those who are shooting—and who will be shot!" (*I* p. 304). Thus, when called upon by fellow *communards* "to put your name there, Vingtras!.," that is, to set fire to a bakery, Vingtras responds, " 'There it is!—and burn down another shack, if needs be!' " (*I* p. 308). In other words, in finally assuming actively the name of the father, Vingtras eschews any compromise with the State apparatus and its bourgeois system of nomination. Rather, he inscribes it actively in the struggle against the system which supported the paternal teaching as well as career-in-teaching, and thereby affirms his "relation to himself" through the "becoming insurgent" and consequent flight from Paris, without resorting to the ultimate mysticism, i.e., the "good peasant sense" of Jean Macquart.

To conclude, I wish to return to *La Débâcle* in order to contrast its dénouement with *L'Insurgé*'s: in both novels, we find *une dernière vision euphorisante* ("a final 'euphorizing' vision"), to use David Baguley's description, but the effect of these images is quite the opposite. As Baguley suggests, Jean's vision "comes to empty out the social and political conflicts in order to assimilate history into nature, for already the order of nature (Jean) has abolished the (dis)order of history."[15] Maurice's death followed by Jean's vision not only eliminates the threshold of focalization for the Commune chapters, but also the vehicle of the novel's historic consciousness—"not only the end of history," says Baguley, "but the debacle of History itself."[16] I would argue further that Zola uses the Commune as an alibi for expounding the salutary political myth with which the cycle of *Les Rougon-Macquart* effectively ends.[17] This moralizing dénouement does not merely reproduce the tendentious ambivalence which characterized Zola's own political writing on the Commune[18] and thus a rather problematic process of subjectivation within history. This strategy also yields a narrative *plissement* of the forces of rupture (Maurice) with those of the natural order (Jean), between which no naming can occur and no locus of subjectivation is textualized other than the gaping abyss in which history and justice can no longer supplant *la fêlure*.[19]

In contrast, the narrative progression in *L'Insurgé* develops the process of *plissement* quite differently. The process of nomination articulates the dispersed field of historical agents, thus avoiding the injustice of their occultation behind a mythic appeal to collective salvation. Furthermore, the protagonist and "author function," Jacques Vingtras, is himself constituted as the locus of knowledge, power, and thought, on the "fold" of history and experience, a process of subjectivation and "becoming insurgé" as marginalized and minor. This "author function" is constantly engaged in an assemblage of conflicts between the subjugated, oppressed group and the enunciative, experimental subject group, always threatened with suppression (as the chapters of Vingtras's flight amply demonstrate), yet always ready for more expressive becomings, even in exile, as revealed in the final chapter, *L'Evasion* ("The Escape"):

> *Bien d'autres enfants ont été battus comme moi, bien d'autres bacheliers ont eu faim, qui sont arrivés au cimetière sans avoir leur jeunesse vengée.*
> *Toi, tu as rassemblé tes misères et tes peines, et tu as amené ton peloton de recrues à cette révolte qui fut la grande fédération des douleurs.*
> *De quoi te plains-tu?* . . . (*I* p. 341)

("Many other children were beaten like me, many other *bacheliers* were hungry, arriving at the cemetery without having had their youth avenged./ You, you have brought together your misery and pain, and you have led your platoon of recruits to this revolt which was the great federation of suffering./ What do you have to complain about?")

But, in contrast to Maurice's embrace of the abyss and to Jean's "extraordinary sensation" of "a dawn" which would bring from "a fury of fate, a cluster of disasters," from "the rubble and the dead in all quarters, . . . an entire world to reconstruct!" (*D* p. 911), Vingtras escapes toward a renewed political commitment:

Je viens de passer un ruisseau qui est la frontière.
Ils ne m'auront pas! Et je pourrai être avec le peuple encore, si le peuple est
rejeté dans la rue et acculé dans la bataille. (I p. 341)

("I just passed a stream that is the border./ They won't capture me! And
I will again be with the people, if the people are thrown into the street and
cornered in battle.")

Then, rather than arriving at a mystical vision of "the rejuvenation of
eternal nature, of eternal humanity" (*D* p. 912), Vingtras's final vision
presents the metaphor of a different "euphoric" horizon, one of
bloody struggle for oppressed subject groups, both past and future:

Je regarde le ciel du côté où je sens Paris.
Il est d'un bleu cru, avec des nuées rouges. On dirait une grande blouse
inondée de sang. (I pp. 340–41)

("I am looking at the sky in the direction that I sense Paris./ It's a harsh
blue, with red clouds. One would say a great tunic soaked in blood.")

With Jean Macquart's final vision, "this great and difficult task of
remaking all of France," Zola does not simply perpetuate the natu-
ralist rejection of politics in the ahistorical devalorization of any cause
that would upset the forces of order and "eternal nature." He also
denies textually the existence of those historical agents at odds with
order and nature, and in so doing, elaborates a revision better suited to
a xenophobic ideological practice rarely associated with the author of
J'Accuse. In contrast, Vallès's efforts to name and thereby articulate an
assemblage of subject positions in history reveal the double play of
"the inside of the outside," folding the historical "moving matter"
into the difficult struggle of a continuous "self-constitution." While
this process is certainly limited in the particular desperation arising
from the repression of the Commune, what remains unlimited, nonetheless, is the potential for becomings, for the inevitable reconstitu-
tion of the subject's "relation to itself" in the *plissement* whose process
is concomitant with those of knowledge and power, but situated on the
fold of thought which forcefully introduces the possibility of resistance and the necessity of history.

Notes

1. Gilles Deleuze, *The Logic of Sense*, trans. Mark Lester with Charles J. Stivale,
ed. Constantin V. Boundas (New York: Columbia University Press, 1990), originally

published as *Logique du sens* (Paris: Minuit, 1969), abbreviated *LS* in the text (the first page number refers to the translation, the second to the French original).

2. Emile Zola, *La Débâcle* in *Les Rougon-Macquart*, Vol. 5 (Paris: Gallimard, Pléiade, 1960), abbreviated D in the text (all translations my own).

3. Gilles Deleuze, *Foucault*, trans. Sean Hand (Minneapolis: University of Minnesota Press, 1988), originally published as *Foucault* (Paris: Minuit, 1986), abbreviated F in the text (the first page number refers to the translation, the second to the French original).

4. David Baguley, "Le Récit de guerre: narration et focalisation dans 'La Débâcle'," *Littérature* 50 (1983): 82–90.

5. Sandy Petrey, "La République de *La Débâcle*," *Les Cahiers naturalistes* 54 (1980): 93 (my translation).

6. On the "indirect mode," see Vaheed K. Ramazani, *The Free Indirect Mode. Flaubert and the Poetics of Irony* (Charlottesville, VA: University Press of Virginia, 1988), 43–50.

7. Naomi Schor, *Zola's Crowds* (Baltimore & London: The Johns Hopkins University Press, 1978), 116.

8. Naomi Schor argues that the introduction of Henriette, "Maurice's fraternal twin (and surrogate mother-protector)," is the necessary "expedient to interrupt the natural course of events," i.e., Zola's rendering explicit the homosexual male bond between Jean and Maurice which progresses toward an impossible consummation. That the relationship between Jean and Henriette itself is never consummated "not only averts a homosexual marriage by proxy, but attests to the profound class divisions which, according to Zola, produced the Commune and its bloody repression." *Ibid.*, 117–118.

9. Philippe Bonnefis, *Vallès: Du bon usage de la lame et de l'aiguille* (Lausanne: L'Age d'Homme, 1982), 95 (my translation).

10. Jules Vallès, *L'Enfant* (Paris: Editeurs français réunis, 1964), abbreviated E in the text; *Le Bachelier* (Paris: Editeurs français réunis, 1955); *L'Insurgé* (Paris: Editeurs français réunis, 1973), abbreviated *I* in the text (all translations are my own).

11. On "subjugated groups" and subject groups," see also Gilles Deleuze and Félix Guattari, *Anti-Oedipus*, trans. Robert Hurley, Mark Seem and Helen R. Lane (New York: Viking, 1977; reprint, Minneapolis: University of Minnesota Press, 1983), 348–50; originally published as *L'Anti-Œdipe, Capitalisme et schizophrénie* I (Paris: Minuit, 1972; 1975), 416–19.

12. The term "author function" (*fonction-auteur*) is proposed by Michel Foucault in "What is an Author?," *Language, Counter-Memory, Practice*, trans. Donald F. Bouchard and Sherry Simon (Ithaca: Cornell University Press, 1977), 113–38, originally published as "Qu'est-ce qu'un auteur?," *Bulletin de la société française de philosophie*, 63.3 (1969): 75–95. For a development of the role of the "author-function" and of the molar and molecular stratification in the Jacques Vingtras Trilogy, see Charles J. Stivale, *Oeuvre de sentiment, oeuvre de combat: La trilogie de Jules Vallès* (Lyon: Presses universitaires de Lyon, 1988).

13. Schor, *Zola's Crowds*, 114.

14. On the onomastic play in the Trilogy, see Charles J. Stivale, "La Signature de Jules Vallés dans la trilogie de *Jacques Vingtras*: Entre autobiographie et fiction," *French Literature Series* XII (1985): 108–11.

15. Baguley, "Récit de guerre," 90 (my translation).

16. *Ibid.*

17. Regarding this "ending," see David Gross, "Emile Zola as Political Reporter in 1871: What He Said and What He Had to Say," *Literature and History* 7 (1978): 34–47;

and David Baguley, "Formes et significations: sur le dénouement de *La Débâcle*," *Cahiers de l'U.E.R. Froissart* 5 (1980): 65–72.

18. Zola's writings on and during the Commune have been studied at some length; see, for example, Pierre Cogny, "Le Discours de Zola sur la Commune: Étude d'un problème de réception," *Les Cahiers naturalistes* 54 (1980): 17–24; Henri Mitterand, *Zola journaliste de l'affaire Manet à l'affaire Dreyfus* (Paris: Armand Colin, 1962), 133–56; Roger Ripoll, "Zola et les Communards," *Europe* 468–69 (1968): 16–26; Rodolphe Walter, "Zola et la Commune: un exil volontaire," *Les Cahiers naturalistes* 43 (1972): 25–37; Henry H. Weinberg, "Zola and the Paris Commune: The *La Cloche* Chronicles," *Nineteenth-Century French Studies* 8.1–2 (1979–1980): 79–86.

19. On "justice" and "naming," see Jean-François Lyotard, *Instructions païennes* (Paris: Galilée, 1977), 16–35; and *Le différend* (Paris: Minuit, 1983), 56–92, trans. as *The Differend. Phrases in Dispute*, trans. Georges Van Den Abbeele (Minneapolis: University of Minnesota Press, 1988), 32–58.

Anti-Semitism and Occultism in *fin-de-siècle* France: Three 'Initiates'

WILLA Z. SILVERMAN

"*[I]ls arrivent on ne sait d'où, ils vivent dans un mystère, ils meurent dans une conjecture . . . Ils ne parviennent pas, ils surgissent tout à coup . . . ; ils ne meurent pas, ils disparaissent brusquement, dans un drame . . .*"[1] ("No one knows where they come from, they live in mystery, they die in conjecture . . . They do not arrive, but surge up suddenly . . . ; they do not die, but disappear brusquely, dramatically. . . .") The subject of this 1896 text is not phantoms, but the Jews, and its author is Edouard Drumont. The so-called 'Pope of anti-Semitism' was not the only extreme-right-wing writer of the late-nineteenth century to link the Jews with an unseen, malevolent realm; nor was he the only one to embrace both anti-Semitism and occultism. Indeed, the occultist craze which captivated *fin-de-siècle* France drew many adepts from the equally thriving literary and political circles of the far right.

Occultism emerged as part of the ideological and literary language of the nationalist right in the last decades of the nineteenth century, furnishing this right with tropes through which it could express its fears and aspirations. Both the Jews and the other world were feared by this anti-Semitic right as menacing, evil powers, harbingers of an imminent apocalypse. This association, of course, was not new; medieval passion plays often depicted the Jews as deicides, devils, and ritual murderers. This view persisted at the end of the century with words such as the Abbé Desportes's 1890 *Le Mystère du sang chez les Juifs (The Jewish Blood Mystery)*.

Yet both anti-Semitism and occultism might also be considered in a specifically *fin-de-siècle* context, as two thrusts of a protean revolt against the late-nineteenth century's dominant secular dogma, scientific materialism. There were more things in heaven and earth, it was realized, than could be explained by positivist philosophy. Nevertheless, magnetists, mesmerists, and other conversants with the supernatural often claimed a parascientific authority shared, for example,

155

with racialist 'ethnologists' like Vacher de Lapouge. Assisted by his faithful sidekick, Paul Valéry, Lapouge was fond of measuring the width of Jewish skulls to 'prove' Jewish 'racial' inferiority.

The Jewish and occult menaces, some argued in late nineteenth-century France, resulted in part from invisibility, from immateriality. Just as spirits remained unseen, yet pervasive, so too were the Jews traditionally depicted as fugitive, nomadic, *errant* (wandering). Furthermore, the Jews's perceived ability, like that of medieval alchemists, to 'create something from nothing' through credit and speculation, made them equally suspect as practitioners of what one might call "voodoo economics." In the case of the Jews and of the occult, appearance belied reality; a simple young girl could suddenly utter remarkable prophecies, just as the relatively small size of French Jewry seemed disproportionate to its purported amazing hold on French society.

This invisible menace, reasoned Drumont and others, needed to be subverted, if necessary by equally irrational and unscientific means. Becoming an 'initiate' provided the weapons necessary to battle occult forces, to form a counterplot to uproot Jewish or occult domination in what had become for many a neo-Darwinian 'struggle for life.'

Writings by three polemical authors, Edouard Drumont, Gaston Méry, and Gyp, illustrate the connections between anti-Semitism and occultism. All three were known for their virulent anti-Semitism and for their dabblings in the occult. And in their essays, journalism, and fiction, all demonstrate a superstitiousness and childish credulity, forms of anti-intellectualism characteristic of both anti-Semitism and occultism.

Edouard Drumont achieved notoriety as author of the 1886 best-selling anti-Semitic breviary, *La France Juive (Jewish France)*, and as founder during the Panama Scandal of the anti-Jewish daily, *La Libre Parole (The Free Word)*. A convert to Catholicism, he placed crucifixes in each office of his newspaper's headquarters. Drumont was also fascinated by the occult. He considered himself an accomplished palmist, often grabbing the hands of new acquaintances to read their palms, and he always carried a mandrake root. He contributed a preface to a work entitled *L'Art divinatoire: les visages et les âmes (The Art of Divination: Faces and Souls)*, whose author attempted to prove that physiognomy revealed destiny. After visiting a psychic who predicted, wrongly, that he would become President of the Republic within ten years, he emerged from her house, according to a friend, "*tout bouleversé*[2] ("completely shaken"). And his belief in turning tables combined utter self-confidence with complete naïveté: "*J'ai vu, comme tout le monde, des tables danser en l'air*"[3] ("I have seen, like everyone else, tables dancing in the air"), Drumont declared, but added that this phenomenon did not seem "particularly exceptional."[4]

In many of Drumont's writings, anti-Semitism meshes with occultism. The occult frequently serves as a metaphor for a type of vague yet unbearable anguish shared by many French people confronting with difficulty the country's transition to modernity. The 1870 defeat and the Commune, French loss of European hegemony, the advent of both a new republican political class and an organized proletariat, technological and scientific progress—to many, Drumont insisted, the world founded on these changes seemed senseless, alien, mysterious. *"Les Français se sentent pris dans quelque chose d'inquiétant et d'obscur"*[5] ("The French feel caught in something unsettling and obscure"), he wrote in *Le Testament d'un antisémite*. And he added: *"La vérité est que nous sommes enveloppés de mystère, que nous vivons dans le mystère"*[6] ("The truth is that we are enveloped in mystery, that we live in mystery"). The 'mystery' of France's brusque transformation, argued Drumont, could not be explained rationally; rather, it was engineered by occult powers, inevitably sinister, inevitably, also, Jewish.

Yet these occult powers, although destructive, remained unseen, and thus almost impossible to subvert. The salons, the press, the army, banking, and industry had all fallen prey to the Jews, he asserted; yet through intermarriage, discreet financial support, spying, and other tactics, their dominion was felt yet not seen. Drumont again evoked occultist images both to describe this 'evil empire' and to express his wish that a few chosen 'initiates' would learn to undo its spell:

> Never has a power been so formidable—and this power rests on nothing; it will collapse, as if by enchantment . . . tomorrow, like those phantasmagoria which disappear in the first morning hours, it will vanish in front of some realistic and sensible people who will confront the phantom and will question it directly. Bizarre power, once again, which is frightening and which, in reality, has no foundation, no body, no apparent existence . . .[7]

This maddening discrepancy between benign appearance and potentially catastrophic reality, suggested Drumont, in fact characterized the entire *fin de siècle*: ". . . *[U]ne fictivité générale . . . est . . . la caractéristique du temps présent"*[8] ("A general fictitiousness . . . characterizes the present age"), he asserted in *La Fin d'un monde* (*The End of a World*). Life had become ironic, in the image of the new ruler of the world, Satan, *"ce roi de l'imposture et de la malfaisante ironie"*[9] ("this king of imposture and harmful irony").

Diabolical powers were indeed responsible for the political and financial scandals of the early Third Republic, Drumont insisted. Writing about the Panama Scandal, he described Cornélius Herz, one of the middlemen accused of bribing deputies, as *"mystérieux comme un alchimiste, impénétrable comme un conspirateur et pratique comme un financier"*[10] ("mysterious as an alchemist, impenetrable as a conspirator, and practical as a financier"). And in a particularly inflammatory editorial written shortly before Esterhazy's January 1898 court-martial, Drumont likened the Dreyfus Affair to a Black Sabbath:

> It is indeed the Sabbath, that is to say, the sacrilegious parody and blasphemy against Truth and Fatherland, a sort of incoherent dance whose circle widens constantly and which little by little draws each person into its delirious movement.[11]

Each member of the Dreyfusard clan, Drumont insisted, participated in this modern Walpurgis Night. Senate Vice-President Scheurer-Kestner, instrumental in bringing Esterhazy to trial, was transformed into *"un vieux satyre, qu'une capiteuse Haïtienne a entraîné dans la clairière par une nuit sans lune"*[12] ("an old satyr, enticed into a glade by a seductive Haitian woman on a night without moonlight"), while historian Gabriel Monod, from a noted Protestant family, *"profane les burettes et souille ce qui est à sa portée"*[13] ("profanes the holy oils and soils whatever is within his reach"). Finally, evoking what Bram Dijkstra has identified as "fantasies of feminine evil in *fin-de-siècle* culture,"[14] Drumont warns of *"sorcières juives [qui] chevauchent sur des manches à balai"*[15] ("Jewish witches [who] ride on broomsticks").

Drumont, of course, did not have a monopoly on the occult during the Dreyfus Affair. Out of desperation, Alfred's brother Mathieu Dreyfus consulted a Norman peasant woman, reputed to have psychic powers. Out of paranoia, Major du Paty du Clam of the army's General Staff disguised himself as a mysterious veiled woman in a meeting with Esterhazy. The forged letters, secret dossiers, and aliases which punctuate the Affair liken it to the bizarre and often macabre experiences of the contemporary fictional adventurer, Rocambole. Drumont referred so constantly to the occult in part out of sincere belief; his writings indicate that he quite literally construed the Dreyfus Affair as an apocalyptic struggle between angels and devils.

Yet Drumont was also a shrewd press magnate, eager to sell newspapers. His readers included many *petit bourgeois* as well as rural clergymen, *curés de campagne*. This audience was both anti-Semitic, for various reasons, and, like many in France at that time, profoundly superstitious. In a country where cases of witchcraft appeared in the courts at least into the 1870s and where Lavisse's new republican textbook needed to warn children against believing in ghosts and the power of amulets,[16] Drumont's blending of anti-Jewish and occult themes was sure to find a following.

Another writer to exploit this potent mix of anti-Semitism and occultism was in fact one of Drumont's collaborators, Gaston Méry. A failed teacher and lawyer, Méry had published several bad novels before joining Drumont's staff at *La Libre Parole*. While not as rabid an anti-Semite as his employer, Méry nevertheless adhered to the doctrine of *"celtisme intégral"* ("integral Celtism") promoted by Jacques de Biez, whose motto was: *"Le méridional, voilà l'ennemi"* ("The southerner, there is the enemy").

The occult also obsessed Méry, who devoured, according to a friend, *"des quantités incroyables"*[17] ("incredible quantities") of spiritist literature. It was Méry who, in 1896, 'discovered' Henriette Couédon, a twenty-three-year-old visionary supposedly inspired by the archangel Gabriel. The day after Méry first reported Couédon's prophecies, he received over a thousand letters requesting her address; soon, the entire Parisian press was detailing her activities, while large crowds, including foreigners from the United States and Spain, lined up outside her home in the Rue de Paradis.

The sensational revelations of Mlle. Couédon provided Méry with enough material to launch his own publication, *l'Echo du merveilleux*, one of the many at the end of the century devoted entirely to the occult.[18] In this bimonthly, described in the first issue as *"la barque qui vous conduira vers les plages miroitantes du surnaturel"*[19] ("the boat which will steer you towards the glistening shores of the supernatural realm"), Méry proposed to report occult phenomena and to stimulate a debate about their existence among scientists, clergy, and spiritists. Haunted houses, twelve-year old mediums, dream interpretation, card reading, vampirism, hypnotism, hallucinations, and photography of the invisible all received periodic attention in the paper. The celebrity psychic of the Rue de Paradis was, of course, observed closely, as were a group of Norman peasant girls who claimed to have sighted the Virgin, and a priest who succeeded in exorcising devils out of children with a special cane. Even a particularly troublesome spirit nicknamed 'le mexicain' proved no contest for this fat, red-faced *abbé*, *"dompteur de diables"*[20] ("devil-tamer").

How do the Jews figure into Méry's discourse on the occult? First, *l'Echo du merveilleux* frequently ran ads for anti-Semitic literature, often published by the Librairie Antisémite. Conversely, Méry's articles on the *voyante* (seer) and the table of contents of his newspaper were regularly published in Drumont's *Libre Parole*. This collaboration between Méry and Drumont in advertising and marketing suggest that they both targeted an audience intrigued and repelled by the occult and by the Jews.

Drumont also prefaced Méry's collected writings on Mlle. Couédon; as in his anti-Semitic pamphlets, Drumont evoked the occult to signify the ominous situation of modern man, precariously balanced on the edge of *"un formidable inconnu [qui] effraie plus qu'il n'attire"*[21] ("a dreadful unknown [which] frightens more than it attracts"). He exhorted Couédon to provide initiation into the secrets of the future, *"un avenir plein d'incertitudes et de mystères"*[22] ("a future full of uncertainties and mysteries").

In the first issue of *l'Echo du merveilleux*, Méry was more explicit than Drumont in identifying the source of late nineteenth-century *angst*. He pointed to *"le péril social"*[23] ("the social peril"), which the Church and Science had been unable to conquer, and which might only be destroyed, he argued, through a new idealism and anti-materialism. In the political rhetoric of the early Third Republic, the phrase *"péril social"* might be read as either the working class or the Jews. Given Drumont and Méry's sometimes maudlin expressions of sympathy for workers, it seems more likely that for them the "social peril" had another, more diabolical origin.

The disclosures of Mlle. Couédon reported in Méry's newspaper reveal another connection between anti-Semitism and occultism. Standing on tiptoe, arms outstretched, Henriette's eyeballs would roll back as she would begin babbling prophecies in seven syllable verses, all ending in "é." Readers learned that France would be chastised for impiety and pride, President Faure would resign and the Opera and Hôtel de Ville would burn. The Jews, chanted Couédon, would also be punished in this apocalyptic scene:

> The Jews will stir about
> I foresee a hectic month
> I foresee troubles
> Those who have speculated
> Will attempt further manipulation
> Some people will plot . . .[24]
> The rope will be drawn
> As in days of yore
> The Stock Exchange will close . . .[25]

The *voyante*'s predictions about the Jews's unhappy fate, meticulously reproduced in Méry's paper, perhaps suggested to credulous readers that the same occult powers the Jews seemed to manipulate to perturb society could in fact be used against them, in this case to forecast their demise. 'Initiates' like Henriette Couédon could indeed succeed in 'turning the tables.' And the process had already begun. Significantly, for several weeks Méry ran a front-page story, found just below the previous day's prophecies, relating Couédon's disputes with her Jewish landlord, who was infuriated that his building had become a tourist mecca. When he threatened to evict her unless she granted him a private session, she refused, vowing she would never open her home to a Jew. Méry's message in these articles was clear: Former 'slaves' had already begun to replace their 'masters.' Occultism at the end of the century thus served as a double-edged sword, allowing some of its adepts to wage war as both victims and aggressors.

A final writer who saw herself as both pawn and potential controller of the occult was the popular novelist, journalist, and playwright known pseudonymously as Gyp. A regular collaborator at *La Libre Parole* and a self-proclaimed 'professional' anti-Semite, Gyp also shared her colleagues' fascination with spiritism. She was a client of the society psychic and graphologist Desbarolles and pronounced herself *"très disposée à croire . . . au merveilleux"*[26] ("very much inclined to believe in . . . the supernatural") in an 1898 survey on the subject printed in Méry's newspaper.

Gyp worked occultist motifs into her 1885 *roman à clefs*, entitled *Le Druide, roman parisien (The Druid, a Parisian Novel)*. This novel, which recreates an attack on Gyp with sulfuric acid by a veiled woman, crudely reveals her paranoia about being the victim of a cabal. And like the discourse of many *fin-de-siècle* spiritists, her novel relies on contrasting images of light and obscurity, truth and secrecy. Even the novel's epigraph encapsulates her obsession with these Manichean dualities. Quoting Octave Mirbeau, she introduces the novel's thesis: *"Si, au lieu de s'acharner, comme on le fait, à cacher les hontes, on les dévoilait d'une façon retentissante, j'imagine que tout n'en irait que mieux"* ("If, instead of striving to hide shameful acts, as is the custom, we unveiled them dramatically, I image that all would work out for the best"). Those guilty of 'veiling' shameful Truths, in Gyp's novel, are all employees of a newspaper called *Le Druide*, a thinly guised version of the popular *fin-de-siècle* daily *Le Gaulois* (The Gaul). Gyp caricatures *Le Gaulois*'s publisher Arthur Meyer—a Jew too assimilated for her tastes—as Anatole Solo, who mysteriously finagled his way into the press *"sous le patronage inexpliqué d'un financier"*[27] ("thanks to the unexplained patronage of a financier"). Solo has hired a Mr. Müller, Germanic in name at least, as his personal spy. Among Solo's henchmen is the caustic journalist Daton, member of a secret society *"qui ne travaille 'ouvertement' que dans certains coins où tu ne vas pas"*[28] ("which only works 'openly' in certain corners where you will never go"). Also on the staff is Geneviève Roland, author of *Le Druide*'s gossipy "Paris-Bloc" column. Roland, the narrator concedes, has a certain beauty. Yet her 'Semiticized' features—*"la peau épaisse, l'oreille canaille, les hanches lourdes, les attaches engorgées"*[29] ("thick skin, coarse ears, heavy haunches, swollen joints"), almost ideographically tip off the reader: Roland, as the rest of the novel reveals, cannot be trusted.

Le Druide thus offers up the anxiety-charged fragments of Gyp's mental universe—anonymous letters, false documents, spies, secret societies, meetings in murky places, aliases, treachery. These images suggest that occultism was not merely a fad enchanting many during the period which also saw the birth of right-wing nationalism in France. Instead, occultism became an integral part of nationalist political rhetoric. Fear of domination by a hidden authority matched a desire to subvert and replace this authority; for both anti-Semitism and occultism are discourses of those excluded from power. Parallelling in some respects the evolution of the nationalist right, a part of the socialist Left, disillusioned by its 1848 defeat, also drifted toward spiritism. Gathered around the séance table, connected to their neighbors by the touch of fingertips, these initiates could claim to form a counter-fraternity, united not to unleash Evil but to reveal divine Truth. Occultism could then become at once both a form of proto-socialism and a 'religion.'

The end of the nineteenth century, then, was not the first period to identify Jews with mysterious evil beings. Nor was it the last. A friend of Gyp's, now an elderly French woman living in Paris, fondly recalled in an interview evenings she had spent around a séance table—during the Occupation, at Vichy.[30]

Notes

1. Edouard Drumont, *De l'or, de la boue, du sang* (Paris, n.d.), 77–78.
2. Raphaël Viau, *Vingt Ans d'antisémitisme: 1889–1909* (Paris, 1910), 111.
3. Edouard Drumont, *La Libre Parole*, 12 November 1897: 1.
4. Ibid.
5. Edouard Drumont, *Le Testament d'un antisémite* (Paris, 1891), viii.
6. Edouard Drumont, *La Dernière Bataille: Nouvelle étude psychologique et sociale* (Paris, n.d.), 517, quoted in Michel Winock, *Edouard Drumont et Cie: Antisémitisme et fascisme en France* (Paris, 1982), 52.
7. *"Jamais puissance ne fut plus formidable—et cette puissance ne tient à rien; elle s'effondrera, comme par enchantement . . . demain, semblable à ces fantasmagories qui disparaissent aux premières heures du matin, elle s'évanouira devant quelques êtres de réalité et de bons sens qui marcheront au-devant du fantôme et qui l'interpelleront directement.*

Puissance bizarre, encore une fois, qui est effrayante et qui, au fond, ne repose sur aucune base, n'a point de corps, n'a pas d'existence apparente . . ."
Edouard Drumont, *La Fin d'un monde: Etude psychologique et sociale* (Paris, 1889), 52.

8. Ibid., 510.

9. Drumont, *Le Testament d'un antisémite,* vii.

10. Drumont, *De l'or, de la boue, du sang,* 68.

11. *"C'est bien le Sabbat, c'est-à-dire la parodie sacrilège et le blasphème contre la Vérité et la Patrie, une sorte de ronde incohérente dont le cercle s'aggrandit sans cesse et qui entraîne peu à peu chacun dans un mouvement délirant."*
Edouard Drumont, "Le Sabbat," *La Libre Parole,* 27 November 1897: 1.

12. Ibid.

13. Ibid.

14. Bram Dijkstra, *Idols of Perversity: Fictions of Feminine Evil in 'Fin-de-Siècle' Culture* (New York and Oxford, Eng., 1986).

15. Drumont, "Le Sabbat," 1.

16. See Eugen Weber, *Peasants into Frenchmen: The Modernization of Rural France, 1870–1914* (Stanford, CA, 1976), 22–29.

17. Viau, *Vingt Ans d'antisémitisme,* 41.

18. A sampling of *fin-de-siècle* spiritist reviews includes: *La Curiosité, l'Etoile, l'Hyperchimie, l'Initiation, l'Isis moderne, Le Journal du magnétisme, Le Lotus bleu, La Lumière, Mélusine, Le Moniteur spirite et magnétique, Le Progrès spirite, La Revue du spiritisme, La Revue spirite,* and *Le Voile d'Isis.*

19. Gaston Méry, *l'Echo du merveilleux,* 15 January 1897: 1.

20. Viau, 147.

21. Edouard Drumont, preface to Gaston Méry, *La Voyante de la rue de Paradis* (Paris, n.d.), iv.

22. Ibid.

23. Gaston Méry, *l'Echo du merveilleux,* 15 January 1897: 1.

24. *Les juifs vont se remuer*
Je vois un mois agité
Je vois des troubles de ce côté
Les gens qui ont agioté
Vont comme y pousser
Des gens vont comploter . . .
From *l'Echo du merveilleux,* 1 February 1898.

25. *La corde sera tirée*
Comme dans les temps passés
La Bourse sera fermée . . .
From *l'Echo du merveilleux,* 15 April 1897.

26. "Enquête sur le merveilleux," *l'Echo du merveilleux,* 15 December 1898.

27. Gyp, *Le Druide, roman parisien* (Paris, 1885), 42.

28. Ibid, 159.

29. Ibid., 129.

30. Interview with Mme. F. M., Paris, 1985.

Contributors

DEAN DE LA MOTTE is Assistant Professor of French at Guilford College. The author of articles on Hugo and Flaubert, he is currently at work on a study of utopia, progress, and narrative in nineteenth-century France.

KAREN L. ERICKSON is Assistant Professor of French at Saint John's University, Collegeville, Minnesota. Her research interests include Flaubert, sacred forms in secular literature, and the relationship between biblical exegetical traditions and literary criticism.

SIMA GODFREY is Associate Professor of French at the University of British Columbia. She has published articles on Baudelaire, Flaubert, Nerval, Gautier, Maupassant and on questions of dandyism and fashionability. She is currently writing a book on the concept of fashionability in nineteenth-century France.

EDWARD K. KAPLAN, Professor of French and Comparative Literature at Brandeis University, has published a translation of *Le Spleen de Paris*, entitled *The Parisian Prowler*, which was awarded the 1990 Louis Galantière Prize for Literary Translation from the American Translators Association. He is also author of *Baudelaire's Prose Poems. The Esthetic, the Ethical and the Religions in "The Parisian Prowler"* and three books on Michelet.

WILL L. MCLENDON is Professor of French (Emeritus) at the University of Houston. The author of *Une ténébreuse carrière sous l'Empire et la Restauration: le Comte de Courchamps* and numerous articles, he has also edited *L'Hénaurme siècle*, a collection of essays on nineteenth-century French literature.

ROY JAY NELSON has taught French literature at the University of Michigan since 1957. He has published two books, *Péguy, poète du sacré* and *Causality and Narrative in French Fiction from Zola to Robbe-Grillet*, as well as many articles on nineteenth- and twentieth-century French literature.

164

FRANC SCHUEREWEGEN is Associate Professor at Antwerp University. The author of *Balzac contre Balzac. Les cartes du lecteur,* he has published articles on eighteenth-, nineteenth- and twentieth-century literature. He is currently working on a book on literature and telecommunications.

PETER SCHOFER is Halverson-Bascom Professor of French at the University of Wisconsin–Madison. He is coauthor of two books—*Poèmes, Pièces, Prose* and *Autour de la littérature*—and of a monograph on rhetorical poetics. He is currently completing a book on Baudelaire.

WILLIAM SHARPE teaches English at Barnard College, Columbia University. His publications include *Unreal Cities: Urban Figuration in Wordsworth, Baudelaire, Whitman, Eliot and Williams* and a collection he coedited, *Visions of the Modern City: Essays in Literature, Art, and History.*

WILLA Z. SILVERMAN is Assistant Professor of French at the Pennsylvania State University. Her research and publications focus on culture and politics at the *fin-de-siècle,* especially during the Dreyfus Affair. She is presently completing a biography of Gyp.

CHARLES J. STIVALE is Associate Professor of French at Wayne State University. The author of *Oeuvre de sentiment, oeuvre de combat: La trilogie de Jules Vallès* and *La Temporalité romanesque chez Stendhal* as well as numerous articles on nineteenth-century French literature, he is currently preparing a monograph on Maupassant.

JEAN-JACQUES THOMAS is Professor of Romance Studies and Literature at Duke University and Chairman of the Department of Romance Studies. His books include *Lire Leiris: essai d'étude poétique d'un fonctionnement analinguistique, Poétique générative, La langue, la poésie, Yves Bonnefoy: A Concordance,* and *La Langue volée.* He is Associate Editor of *Sub-Stance* and *Poetics Today.*

JEFFREY WALLEN is Assistant Professor of Comparative Literature at Hampshire College. He has published essays on nineteenth-century French and British writers such as Flaubert, Pater, and Wilde. He is currently working on a study of literary portraiture.

Index